# Pedagogy of the Oppressed

## Also available from Bloomsbury

*Education for Critical Consciousness*, Paulo Freire
*Pedagogy in Process*, Paulo Freire
*Pedagogy of Hope*, Paulo Freire
*Pedagogy of the City*, Paulo Freire
*Pedagogy of the Heart*, Paulo Freire
*The Student Guide to Freire's "Pedagogy of the Oppressed,"* Antonia Darder
*A Pedagogy of Faith*, Irwin Leopando
*Paulo Freire,* Daniel Schugurensky
*Paulo Freire's Intellectual Roots*, Robert Lake and Tricia Kress

### Bloomsbury Critical Education series (series editor: Peter Mayo)

*Pedagogy, Politics and Philosophy of Peace*, Carmel Borg and Michael Grech
*Critical Human Rights, Citizenship, and Democracy Education,* Michalinos
Zembylas and André Keet

### Critical Pedagogy Today series (series editors: Shirley R. Steinberg and Ana Maria Araújo Freire)

*On Critical Pedagogy*, Henry A. Giroux
*Critical Pedagogy for Social Justice*, John Smyth
*Echoes from Freire for a Critically Engaged Pedagogy*, Peter Mayo
*Critical Narrative as Pedagogy*, Ivor Goodson and Scherto Gill
*Teaching as the Practice of Wisdom*, David Geoffrey Smith

# Pedagogy of the Oppressed
# 50th Anniversary Edition

Paulo Freire

Translated by Myra Bergman Ramos

With an Introduction by Donaldo Macedo
and an Afterword by Ira Shor

BLOOMSBURY ACADEMIC
NEW YORK · LONDON · OXFORD · NEW DELHI · SYDNEY

Bloomsbury Academic
Bloomsbury Publishing Inc
1385 Broadway, New York, NY 10018, USA
50 Bedford Square, London, WC1B 3DP, UK
29 Earlsfort Terrace, Dublin 2, Ireland

BLOOMSBURY, BLOOMSBURY ACADEMIC and the Diana logo
are trademarks of Bloomsbury Publishing Plc

First published 2018
Reprinted 2020, 2021 (twice), 2022

© Paulo Freire, 1970, 1993, and contributors, 2018
Introduction © Donaldo Macedo 2018
Afterword © Ira Shor 2018

Cover design by Clare Turner

A catalog record for this book is available from the Library of Congress.

ISBN: HB: 978-1-5013-1414-8
PB: 978-1-5013-1413-1
ePDF: 978-1-5013-1416-2
ePub: 978-1-5013-1415-5

Typeset by Deanta Publishing Services, Chennai, India
Printed and bound in the United States of America

To find out more about our authors and books visit www.bloomsbury.com
and sign up for our newsletters.

*To the oppressed,*
*and to those who suffer with them*
*and fight at their side*

# Contents

## Chapter 4      125

Antidialogics and dialogics as matrices of opposing theories of cultural action: the former as an instrument of oppression and the latter as an instrument of liberation; the theory of antidialogical action and its characteristics: conquest, divide and rule, manipulation, and cultural invasion; the theory of dialogical action and its characteristics: cooperation, unity, organization, and cultural synthesis

# Introduction to the
# 50th Anniversary Edition

Donaldo Macedo, University of Massachusetts Boston, USA

*A day after New York City came up with a $1,000 bagel, a local restaurateur unveiled a $27,000 chocolate sundae . . . setting a Guinness world record for the most expensive dessert.*

Reuters Business News, November 7, 2007[1]

It is indeed an honor to write the introduction to Paulo Freire's *Pedagogy of the Oppressed*, a book that is unquestionably a classic as it has, throughout this last half century, become increasingly more relevant as the twenty-first century ushers the world into a very dark new age. Leading intellectuals such as Noam Chomsky, Zygmunt Bauman, Henry Giroux, Arundhati Roy, Amy Goodman, Thomas Piketty, among others, have wisely and incessantly alerted people around the world of the dire consequences (i.e., denial of climate change, obscene economic inequality, potential nuclear catastrophe) of the far-right power hegemony that, if left unchecked, may potentially result in the end of humanity as we know it. Thus, not only must an alternative political course be taken, but central to its agenda must also be the development of people's critical awareness of how they are in the world and with the world—a posture that Freire insisted upon and which informed his brilliant and insightful ideals in *Pedagogy of the Oppressed*. That is to say, Freire's major goal in *Pedagogy of the Oppressed* was not to propose an innovative methodology (which would be antithetical to his critique of formulaic models of education) but to launch the development of an emancipatory pedagogical process that invites and challenges students, through critical literacies, to learn how to negotiate the world in which they find themselves, in a thoughtful and critically reflective manner, so as to expose and engage the tensions and contradictions inherent in the ongoing relations between the oppressor and the oppressed. Thus, the central goal of Freire's *Pedagogy of the Oppressed* is to awaken in the oppressed the knowledge, creativity, and constant critical reflective capacities necessary to unveil, demystify, and understand the power relations responsible for their oppressed marginalization and, through this recognition, begin a project of liberation through praxis which, invariably, requires consistent, never-ending critical reflection and action. Currently, while more and more educators are embracing Freire, many of them, including some liberal and progressives, allow their critical discourse to be betrayed by a lack of coherence between their denouncement of oppressive conditions and their accommodation to dominant structures that created these oppressive structures in the first place, a point to which I will return later.

Approximately a month or so before Paulo Freire's untimely death on May 2, 1997, he and I were walking on New York's Fifth Avenue, discussing the obvious contradictions of New York City's opulence that makes it possible for people to flaunt their wealth, for instance, paying $27,000 for a chocolate sundae in luxurious restaurants amid thousands and thousands of homeless people, including families with children who sleep in cars, under bridges, and in overcrowded shelters. The unpacking of these contradictions was to be the major goal of a course that Freire and I were contracted to co-teach at the Harvard Graduate School of Education in fall 1997. We had agreed that we would invite students into a critical dialogue about bodies of knowledges not usually emphasized in the academy such as ethics, the substantivity of democracy beyond the four-year-of-the-carnivalesque voting cycle (as we have recently witnessed with Donald Trump's successful campaign for the presidency), and a rigorous study of ideology and its role in reading the word and the world. During our walk along Fifth Avenue, Freire would frequently ask me if we could stop so he could more emphatically make his points and share his concerns regarding the destructive and oppressive forces of neoliberalism in developed and developing countries. Frequently, we would lean against the wall of imposing buildings to avoid the usual frantic torrent of hurried people who, in a dizzying way, wanted to forge ahead of the other pedestrians, those perhaps who, on occasion, may have slowed down a bit to satisfy their consumerist curiosity at the unending and seductive store window displays of fashion and the latest technological gadgets—a hallmark of an obsessively consumerist society—a society where "money is the measure of all things, and profit the primarily goal. For the oppressors, what is worthwhile is to have more—always more—even at the cost of the oppressed having less or having nothing. For them, *to be* is to have . . ." (p. 58). In retrospect, I now realize that Freire's frequent requests to stop had more to do with the fatigue he was experiencing due to his heart condition—an ailment that he very much kept to himself and about which he seldom complained.

While Freire always remained true to his view of history as possibility and maintained an unflinching hope that a less discriminatory, more just, less dehumanizing, and more humane world is possible, he was always critical of the "libertarian propaganda . . . [that] merely 'implant' in the oppressed a belief in freedom, thus thinking to win their trust."[2] Accordingly, Freire believed that "the correct method lies in dialogue . . . [a process that unveils] . . . the conviction of the oppressed that they must fight for their liberation [which] is not a gift bestowed by the revolutionary leadership, but the result of their own *conscientização*."[3] During this long and engaging walk, Freire shared with me, semi-joking, that the "ruling class will never send us to Copa Cabana for a vacation. If we want to go to Copa Cabana, we have to fight for it." In this last long walk and dialogue with Freire, he would often reveal his frustration that, at times, bordered on "just ire" as he would often say, relative to the accommodation of some turncoat progressives to the neoliberal theology. Such was the case of his friend, the former president of Brazil, Fernando Henriques, who like Freire, had been

exiled to Chile by Brazil's brutal neo-Nazi military dictatorship
that killed and tortured thousands of Brazilians. In fact, Brazil's
experimentation with neoliberalism under the government of
Fernando Henriques exacerbated already cruel conditions and
sentenced millions of Brazilians to hunger, human misery, and
despair which, in turn, contributed to the widening of the economic
and educational inequality gap while unleashing more systemic
government corruption. Sadly, most socialist governments in the
Western world of that time betrayed their commitment to social
justice, equality, and equity by veering toward a neoliberal market-
crazed ideology which not only crushed the hope of people who
aspired for a better world but also brought down the governments
by enabling obscene corruption, as was the case in Portugal, Spain,
and Greece. In the latter country, the socialist party, led by Prime
Minister George Papandreou, allowed corruption to reach epidemic
proportions to the point where, for example, the PASOK would
buy votes by offering free airfare tickets to Greek citizens living the
United States who were willing to fly to Greece with the promise
of voting for the socialists. Such acts smack of the tactics that
Western democracies routinely criticize as the fraudulent election
rigging they say plague those countries pejoratively termed "Third
World Banana Republics." To a degree, socialist governments in
multiple continents fell from power due to obscene scandals of
corruption which, in general, gave rise to center-right and far-right
governments (Greece is an exception where the radical left Syriza
party won the election) that have now been elected by dissatisfied
and disenfranchised voters—voters who became the victims of the
austerity measures imposed by neoliberal policies.

Freire also did not hesitate to demonstrate his "just ire" by
denouncing the critical posture of many facile liberals and some
so-called critical educators who often find refuge in the academy
by hiding their addiction to obscene consumerism, while at the
same time attacking in their written critical discourses the market
theology of neoliberalism. Too often, these facile liberals and
so-called critical educators' tastes and ways of being in the world

and with the world remain, according to Freire, wedded to the very neoliberal market solutions that they denounce at the level of written critical discourse. In their day-to-day practices, these facile liberals and so-called critical educators often betray the action required by praxis by fossilizing their purported political project into an obscure discursive criticality that begs to move beyond the always "postponed arrival" of action—that is, action designed to transform the current perniciousness of the neoliberal Godification of the market into new democratic structures that lead to equity, equality, and authentic democratic practices. In other words, many facile liberals and so-called critical educators boast of their leftist credentials by wearing their proclaimed Marxism on their sleeve (usually only expressed in written discourse or in the safety of the academy) and, sometimes, feel the urge to further boast that, for example, their radicalism is beyond Marx's proposals to the degree that they are authentically more Maoist in their political orientation—a posture they believe to be even more radical. As a consequence, leftist labels in the academy become an appropriated, exoticized political and cultural currency where to be a Marxist-in-residence in the ivory tower bestows status but is little more than a chic brand—in reality, the epitome of consumerism sustained by transactions occurring in a merely symbolic register of names and labels that are otherwise vacuous in substance. In essence, the academic branding of "Marxist" by some critical educators turns ethical and political action into a spectacle, and leftist viewpoints into de facto commodities. As commodities, these self-ascribed "radical" positions and labels are emptied out of their progressive content to the extent that they are decoupled from principled action—a decoupling that remains fundamental in the reproduction of the market theology of neoliberalism where collective social engagement based on critical thinking is discouraged and zealous cutthroat competition is rewarded. The insidious process of decoupling critical discourse and action legitimizes not "walking the talk": it affords the proclaimed Marxist-in-residence the opportunity, for instance, to claim to be antiracist while turning antiracism into a lifeless cliché that does not provide pedagogical spaces to critique white supremacist ideologies. In this process, their progressive stances are often co-opted, mobilized only to the degree that they denounce racism at the level of written critical discourse, all the while reaping privileges from the cemented institutional racism which they, willfully, refuse to acknowledge and engage in action to dismantle.

Hence, these Marxists-in-residence also ignore the political and systemic impact of racism that was amply witnessed in the 2016 US presidential campaign and which became more frightening with each calculated pronouncement by Donald Trump used to ignite white rage against people rather than against the state, for conditions caused, in large part, by the neoliberal policies that the enraged white working class ironically embrace. The election of Trump as president has, in essence, unveiled the lie behind the post-race slogan which proclaimed that "racism is over"—a slogan that took shape with the election of Barack Obama, the first black president. Furthermore, the very failure to acknowledge the ravages of racism while enlarging ghettos, normalizing the school-to-prison pipeline made up mostly of blacks and Latinas(os), and expanding human misery as a by-product of racism, constitutes, in itself, a racist act. It is racism when these proclaimed Marxists and Maoists-in-residence proselytize against racism as an abstract idea and resist the intellectual and societal pressure to translate this abstract idea at the level of written critical discourse into action that would racially democratize society and its institutions. How racially democratic are, for example, the universities, when most departments remain practically all white lest for token professors of color and a miniscule number of non-white students? For instance, does race play a role in the almost non-existence of African Americans in Classics departments both at the faculty and student levels, or is it the case that African Americans are genetically wired to have no vocation toward the study of Classics and are, consequently, averse to Classical studies? More pernicious yet is when these self-proclaimed leftists-in-residence engage in the social construction of not seeing the ingrained racism in their statements and in their behavior. For example, take the case of a proclamation made by a liberal white professor working in an urban university that prides itself for its diversity: "We just want these Black kids to learn how to learn." Such a remark not only points to a rigidly ethnocentric notion of the act of knowing as insightfully argued by Freire in *Pedagogy of the Oppressed*, but it also shows that individuals making such statements remain shackled by white supremacist ideology that has inculcated in them myths and beliefs that children from certain races and cultures are innately incapable of learning until they receive the recipes taught to the poor and the oppressed by educators who often carry, in their leather Gucci bags or briefcases, these prepackaged lesson plans to teach, for example, African Americans what they cannot already know because they have never even had the capacity to acquire knowledge until then. The very survival of the cruel conditions in which these non-white children have been condemned to live demonstrates that they know very well how to learn in order to stay alive in circumstances of "savages inequalities" as poignantly described by Jonathan Kozol in several of his books. Would the daughters and sons of these Marxist-in-residence educators survive the ravages of such entrenched social inequalities and remain unscathed while excelling in the required high-stakes testing? Probably not. Hence, the very survival from the most horrendous forms of racism, segregation, gender and class discrimination not only point to a high level of intelligence of children who are ghettoized but would add credence to Howard Gardner's notion of multiple intelligence beyond the Western-centric notions of "intelligence."

The "just ire" that Freire demonstrated in his last dialogue with me, when he denounced some critical educators who inhabit "silk underwear," was, in turn, channeled by him as a creative force toward the end of his life, both in his writings, as exemplified by his last book *Pedagogy of Freedom*, and in his many later dialogues and lectures throughout the world. Freire correctly opposed the pseudo-critical educator whose political project of social justice is betrayed by intellectual incoherence and a crass careerism fueled by what Freire often called the "ethics" of the market under neoliberalism. In other words, the intellectual incoherence of many critical educators ultimately defines and confines their political project into mere neoliberal crass careerism. However, it is important to point out that Freire's disgust with the crass careerist does not mean that he was against the pursuit of a career. There is a marked difference between having a career that is not instrumentalist and which is situated within a political project that strives for a world that, as Freire would often say, is more round, less unjust, and more democratic, and a careerist whose political project is his or her own individual advancement, marked by sophistry and obscene greed which almost always sacrifice equity, equality, and authentic democracy. That is to say, the careerist's political project is, ultimately, his or her career, and to save his or her career, the crass careerist "will fail to initiate (or will abandon) dialogue, reflection, and communication, and will fall into using slogans, communiqués, monologues, and instructions. Superficial conversions to the cause of liberation carry this danger."[4] The danger lies, for example, in the disarticulation of writing about hunger within the confines and safety of the academy and the actual experience of hunger, or in making the sloganized proclamation "I am a Maoist" while refusing to de-Guccify and allowing oneself to remain shackled to bourgeois values that undergird much of the neoliberal project and which deem the appropriation and accumulation of things as more important than the expansion of humanity. As Freire insightfully argued in *Pedagogy of the Oppressed*, "the liberation of the oppressed is a liberation of women and men, not things. Accordingly, while no one liberates [herself or] himself by [her or] his own efforts alone, neither is [she or] he liberated by others. Liberation, a human phenomenon, cannot be achieved by semihumans. Any attempts to treat people as semihumans [as is the case with White supremacy and patriarchy] only dehumanizes them."[5] A semihuman whose only concern is things and not people can never, nor is he or she willing to, offer a form of literacy that leads to liberation and emancipation. Quite to the contrary, a semihuman who pursues the process of *othering* human beings so as to devalue and typecast them has already lost his or her humanity to the extent the he or she cannot see humanity in others. Accordingly,

> For Freire literacy was not a means to prepare students for the world of subordinated labor or "careers," but a preparation for a self-managed life. And self-management could only occur when people have fulfilled three goals of education: self-reflection, that is, realizing the famous poetic phrase, "know thyself," which is an understanding of the world in which they live, in its economic, political and, equally important, its psychological dimensions. Specifically "critical" pedagogy helps the learner become aware of the forces that have hitherto ruled their lives and especially shaped their consciousness. The third goal is to help set the conditions for producing a new life, a new set of arrangements where power has been, at least in tendency, transferred to those who literally make the social world by transforming nature and themselves.[6]

Because Freire was often criticized for not critically addressing issues of race relations in *Pedagogy of the Oppressed*, one of his major goals in the course that we were going to co-teach at Harvard Graduate College of Education in 1997 was to expand our dialogue titled, "A Dialogue: Culture, Language, and Race," which had been published by *Harvard Educational Review*.[7] In this dialogue, Freire, in a self-critique, explained why class oppression preoccupied him more than race relations when he wrote *Pedagogy of the Oppressed*, given the historical context that shaped oppression in Brazil—an oppression experienced by Freire and his family who lost their middle-class status and had to move from the city and live in the poor, lower-class area named Morro da Saúde. Freire's denunciation of oppression did not constitute a mere intellectual exercise that we often find among many facile liberals and pseudo-critical educators. His intellectual brilliance and courage in denouncing the structures of oppression were rooted in a very real and material experience, as he recounts his childhood and adolescent years living in poverty in Morro da Saúde. The experience of hunger as a child, of a formerly middle-class family that had lost its economic base, enabled Freire to, on the one hand, identify and develop "solidarity with the children from the poor outskirts of town"[8] and, on the other hand, to realize that "in spite of the hunger that gave us solidarity . . . in spite of the bond that united us in our search for ways to survive—our playtime, as far as the poor children were concerned, ranked us as people from another world who happened to fall accidentally into their world."[9] It is the realization of such class borders that led, invariably, to Freire's radical rejection and denunciation of a class-based society.

Although some strands of postmodernism would dismiss Freire's detailed class analysis in *Pedagogy of the Oppressed*, it is an enormous mistake, if not academic dishonesty, to pretend that we now live in a classless world. Although Freire understood very well that "material oppression and the affective investments that tie oppressed groups to the logic of domination cannot be grasped in all of their complexity within a singular logic of class struggle,"[10] he consistently argued that a thorough understanding of oppression must always take a detour through some form of class analysis. At the same time, a postmodern posture that overcelebrates identity politics not only leads to essentialism but also contains within it seeds of oppression. Take for example, the progressive Massachusetts senator Elizabeth Warren's claim to be American Indian even though she is many generations removed from American Indian ancestry and grew up as white and was totally removed from the oppressive life of reservations. Senator Warren's opportunistic use of the race card to make herself more attractive as a candidate for a professorial position at Harvard Law School, and Harvard University's use of her employment as proof of its commitment to diversity, only demonstrates how dominant institutions rely on tokenism to reinforce their exclusionary policies that do not welcome the presence of non-white groups in their institutions other than as token representatives. In reality, the opportunistic use of racial or gender cards defang the very spirit of the Civil Rights Act. It also provides segregationists and those beholden by patriarchy and white supremacy with ammunition to dismiss and criticize the anti-discriminatory laws that discourage exclusion on the base of race or gender.

Until his death, Freire courageously denounced the neoliberal position that promotes the false notion of the end of history and the end of class. In contrast to the idea that society has reached the end point of its evolution, thus emptying history of its meaning, Freire always viewed historical awareness as an ongoing condition for human betterment, opening up the possibility of a better future when "recognizing that History is time filled with possibility and not inexorably determined—that the future is problematic and not already decided, fatalistically."[11] In like manner, Freire continued to reject any false claim to the end of class struggle. Whereas he continually revised his earlier class analyses, he never abandoned or devalued class as an important theoretical category in our search for a better comprehension of conditions of oppression. In the long dialogue we had during his last visit to New York— in fact, the last time we worked together—he restated this view that although one cannot reduce everything to class, class remains an important factor in our understanding of multiple forms of oppression. While poststructuralists may want to proclaim the end of class analysis, they still have to account for the horrendous human conditions that led, as Freire recounted, a family in northeast Brazil to scavenge for food in a landfill and take "pieces of an amputated human breast with which they prepared their Sunday lunch."[12]

Even though I experienced the great good fortune of working with Paulo for sixteen uninterrupted years, first translating many of his books into English and later collaborating with him on other book projects, and I have read and reread the *Pedagogy of the Oppressed* so many times, with each rereading of this book I gain new insights in my understanding of our current world—a world that is plagued by manufactured wars, expanding human misery, and obscene greed. Without falling into false modesty, I have always felt I understood Freire's leading ideas, the subtleties, and the nuances that characterized the *Pedagogy of the Oppressed*. But I did not really fully capture the layered complexity of Freire's philosophy until I visited Morro da Saúde, an impoverished community on the outskirts of Recife in northeast Brazil.

As mentioned earlier, Freire and his family had moved there after the great economic crash of the 1930s that unceremoniously yanked the middle-class rug from under Freire's family. No longer able to afford housing in Recife as the economic situation worsened, Freire's family moved to a modest house in Morro da Saúde where Paulo, his siblings, his parents, and other close family members took refuge. I immediately began to see new dimensions and the raison d'etre of *Pedagogy of the Oppressed*. As I entered the modest house, its dark small rooms, without an indoor bathroom and with non-existent ceilings, I began to put into perspective the traumas that must have overwhelmed Freire as he came face to face with a new form of schooling called life—life created and sustained by a cruel system that uncaringly relegated millions and millions of Brazilians to half citizenry and sub-humanity. I also took a short walk along a shrinking river where Freire and his friends used to take baths alongside the neighborhood women who would religiously wash clothes on a daily basis. The sun was the only towel available to Freire to dry his skin.

Freire learned quickly that a psychological class wall enveloped his new reality as he began to get acquainted with his new friends and neighbors—their humanity enabled him to empathize with his aunt Natércia's preoccupation with keeping their poverty "hidden" and to understand "why the family would not let go of Lourdes's German piano or [his] father neckties,"[13] even when his father was doing manual chores in the workshop. But Freire soon learned that his family's clinging to middle-class markers and mores did little to alleviate their pain—"a pain almost always treated with disrespectful language . . . [as his mother, who would be denied groceries on credit since the family was never able to pay] would leave the shop to look for another one, where new offenses were almost always added to these already suffered."[14] In an effort to protect his mother from such daily blows to her dignity, Freire would often wander into the backyards of neighbors to steal chickens that would frequently be that day's only family meal, since by then all of the town's merchants had refused to grant his family credit. To protect his family's middle-class sensitivities, Freire would euphemize his backyard thefts as "incursions into a neighbor's yard." Freire's mother was a Christian Catholic who no doubt viewed such "incursions" as violations of her moral principles, but she must have realized that "her alternatives were either to reproach [Freire] severely and make [him] return the still warm chicken to [their] neighbors or to prepare the fowl as a special dinner. Her common sense prevailed. Still silent, she took the chicken, walked across the patio, entered the kitchen, and lost herself in doing a job she had not done in a long time."[15] Freire's mother knew that stealing a neighbor's chicken was morally wrong and constituted a crime, but she also knew that there was an *a priori* crime committed by society: the manufacturing of hunger. As Freire recounted,

> The problem of hunger [created by social inequality] . . . was real and concrete hunger that [had] no specific date of departure . On the contrary, our hunger was the type that arrives unannounced and unauthorized, making itself at home without end in sight. A hunger that, if it was not softened as ours was, would take over our bodies, molding them into angular shapes. Legs, arms, and fingers become skinny. Eye sockets become deeper, making the eyes almost disappear. Many of our classmates experienced this hunger and today it continues to afflict millions of Brazilians who die of its violence every year.[16]

It is against this form of violence that Freire angrily and compassionately wrote *Pedagogy of the Oppressed*. In fact, I honestly believe that *Pedagogy of the Oppressed* would not have been written without Freire's class dislocation and the experience of hunger. The reading and rereading of Freire's insights after I visited his humble home in Morro da Saúde, both his denunciation of dehumanizing conditions and his announcement that "change is difficult but possible," unleashed in me a complex of emotions wrought with the reconfirmation of a tremendous loss in his death—a loss infused with "anguish, doubt, expectation, and sadness."[17] At the same time, with each new publication of Freire's unpublished work and publications about his theories regarding the liberation of women and men, "we can celebrate in joy [Freire's] return"[18] as he, over and over again, energizes and challenges us to imagine a world that is less cruel, more just, and more democratic. However, as Freire so energetically insisted in his writings, the announcement of a more just and humane world must always be preceded by the denunciation of the dominant forces that generate, inform, and shape discrimination, human misery, and dehumanization. Hence, the denunciation of oppressive societal forces cannot be done through mere instructional methodologies that anesthetize and domesticate the mind, through banal information transmission that Freire termed as "banking" education. Yet Freire's condemnation of mere methods continues to be misappropriated and distorted. There is deep irony in some academics' efforts to interrogate whether Freire's *methods* work and to apologetically provide examples of Freirean schools that *do work*, as Howard Gardner did in a panel discussion on Freire with Noam Chomsky and Bruno de la Chiesa which took place at Harvard in May 2013 as part of an *Askwith Forum*, thus vulgarizing Freire's intellectual contributions and his major theories. To reduce Freire's leading theoretical and philosophical ideas to a method in such an overt manner is to demonstrate that Gardner's touted theory of "multiple intelligence" is susceptible to narrow mindedness, particularly when Freire's theories are dismissed as "irrelevant"—a dismissal clearly shaped and controlled by ideology. Therefore, the demand posed by Gardner to Noam Chomsky, Bruno de la Ciesa, and the *Forum*'s audience to provide concrete examples which demonstrate that

Freire's method itself works[19] hides more than it elucidates. The real question regarding Freire's ideas and theories in *Pedagogy of the Oppressed* is whether it is correct to view Freire's literacy proposals as mere instructional methods, as Noam Chomsky responded to Gardner during the *Forum*. According to Chomsky, Freire used literacy "as a means to consciousness raising."[20] Simply put, Chomsky was urging educators in general, and critical educators in particular, to move beyond the fetishization of methods that so paralyzes thinking, innovation, and creativity among North American educators, a phenomenon insightfully analyzed by Lilia I. Bartolomé in her classic article, "Beyond the Methods Fetish: Toward a Humanizing Pedagogy," published by the Harvard Educational Review.[21]

Consequently, Freire has to be viewed and understood beyond his literacy instructional methods by critically apprehending his notion of *conscientization*—a concept that is often misunderstood even by critical educators who claim to be Freirean, and conveniently dismissed by educators whose interest is to appropriate Freire's dialogical method disarticulated from Freire's major theoretical goal thus reducing him to a mere instructional methodologist. In addition to "methods fetish" of many educators, one of the challenges of defining Freire's original concept, *conscientização*, lies in the difficulty of pronouncing a Portuguese word (Portuguese speakers also experience varied difficulty pronouncing it), and also in the fact that most definitions of this insightful concept rarely do justice to what Freire had in mind. Freire always insisted that before we even attempt to define *conscientização*, we need to adhere to the essence of this concept and ask: "What definition, against what, for whom, and against whom?" If we begin to answer these questions we soon realize that, even for many followers of Freire's thinking, *conscientização* presents a certain difficulty beyond the hurdles of its correct pronunciation—being a term that Freire, at least initially, refused to have translated into English by simply stating: "I refuse. Why not accept this term? I do not have to accept *stress*, but I have. Why do you not accept *conscientização*?"[22] Freire eventually agreed to have his term translated into the approximate English translation: *conscientization.*

For Freire, the demystification of *conscientization* would necessarily have to include the reclaiming of the oppressed's own words as a process of coming to voice, which he viewed as "the fundamental theme of the Third World—implying a difficult but not impossible task for its people—[which] is the conquest of its right to voice, of the right to pronounce its word."[23] It is this right that the oppressed need to reclaim in order to speak their word, "the right to be [themselves], to assume direction of [their] destiny."[24] It is this right that the dominant forces go to great lengths to suffocate, seeking to sequester the words of the oppressed—words that unveil the mechanism of oppression and are distorted or repressed, as Henry Giroux suggests, in "a society that revels in bouts of historical and social amnesia [in which] it is much easier for the language of politics and community to be stolen and deployed like a weapon so as to empty words such as democracy, freedom, justice and the social state of any viable meaning."[25] The sequestration of language by dominant forces of oppression, and even by liberal educators who proselytize about "empowering minorities" and "giving them voice" when they themselves represent the majority, is evident in the overuse and abuse of euphemisms in academic discourses and mainstream media.

Euphemism is a form of language that not only mystifies and distorts reality; it is also a much-used technique by dominant forces (the media, political pundits, the educated class) to distract attention from the real issues that ail society, such as the obscene widening of the income gap between the rich and the poor, the pernicious shrinking of the middle-class, and the generalized alienation of the dispossessed. The suppression or distortion of language is a tactic that, according to Arundhati Roy, also appears as

> usurping words and deploying them like weapons . . . using them to mask intent and to mean exactly the opposite of what they have traditionally meant has been one of the most brilliant strategic

victories of czars of the new dispensation. It has allowed them to
marginalize their detractors, deprive them of a language to voice
their critique.[26]

When the technique of sequestration fails to work, the dominant
forces engage in more draconian measures, as was evident when
a Tucson Public Schools official in Arizona banned Freire's
*Pedagogy of the Oppressed* from classrooms because, according to
a superintendent of the Arizona Department of Education, "We
should not be teaching [kids] . . . that they're oppressed."[27] In other
words, *conscientization*—as a process to acquire the necessary
critical thinking tools so that students, instead of internalizing
their oppression, understand how institutions of power work to
deny them equality of treatment, access, and justice—is not a goal
of Tucson Public Schools, where courses that deal with issues such
as race relations, ethics, and ideology are banned and teachers
are encouraged to promote a pedagogy of big lies through which
students (in this case, lower-class Mexican-American students)
can be more easily domesticated. The almost total lack of public
outcry in the United States regarding the censorship of books and
the heisting of language that names reality in order to contest
oppression "may prove to be the keystone of our undoing."[28]
I am amazed to witness academics engage in euphemisms as
they aggressively object to any discourse that both fractures the
dominant language and lays bare the veiled reality in order to
name it. It is still more amazing to witness educators who claim to
be Freirean fail to see the obvious impossibility of the oppressed
apprehending through the process of *conscientization*, "a deepened
consciousness of their situation . . . as an historical reality susceptible
of transformation"[29] while these liberal educators remain complicit
in the erasure of language—an act that empties out, for example,
the meaning of the term "oppressed." Many of these liberals eagerly
embrace euphemisms such as "disadvantaged," "disenfranchised,"
"economically marginal," "minority," and "at-risk," among others, to
refer to the oppressed, but in doing so obfuscate the true historical

conditions that explain "'the here and now,' which constitutes the situation within which [the oppressed] are submerged, from which they emerge, and [in] which they intervene"[30] to denounce and confront their oppressors in their "pursuit of full humanity."[31] This sequestration of language denies people the possibility to understand the dialectical relationship between the oppressor and the oppressed. If you have an oppressed, you must have an oppressor.

Thus, language is not only a site of contestation; it is also an indispensable tool for a critical reflexive demystification process that is central to *conscientization*—a process which Freire refuses to vulgarize and reduce to mere methods to be consumed by the so-called First World progressive educators who, in many instances, remain chained to the "mystification of methods and techniques and, indeed, a reduction of *conscientization* to certain methods and techniques used in Latin America for adult literacy."[32] Hence, Freire's major goal as I had mentioned earlier was not to develop a literacy methodology to be used universally with oppressed people of the world. His main goal was to use literacy and the subsequent methods he developed for particular groups of adult learners to lead people to *conscientization*. In other words, no matter where we come from,

> all of us are involved in a permanent process of *conscientization*, as thinking beings in a dialectical relation with an objective reality upon which we act. What varies in time and space are the contents, methods, and objectives of *conscientization* . . . [when human beings became aware] and made themselves capable of revealing their active reality, knowing it and understanding what they know.[33]

Another critical misunderstanding of *conscientization* is to view the concept "as a kind of tropical exoticism, a typically Third World entity. People speak of *conscientization* as an inviable goal for 'complex societies,' as though the Third World nations were not complex in their own way."[34] This false dichotomy between the so-called First World and Third World represents yet another sequestration of language designed to lead to a form of mystification—a distraction that functions as a reproductive mechanism designed to create a center or a core of romanticized Eurocentric values while relegating other cultural expressions to the margins. The current attacks on Islam and on Muslims in general are a case in point where Western media, political pundits, and academics often totalize religio-cultural extremists and generalize the extremism to all Muslims, framing them all as potential terrorists. At the same time, we conveniently ignore extremists of the West like evangelist Pat Robertson, who camouflages his bigotry and his constant attacks on women. Take, for example, Robertson's statement that "the feminist agenda is not about equal rights for women. It is about a socialist, anti-family political movement that encourages women to leave their husbands, kill their children, practice witchcraft, destroy capitalism and become lesbians."[35] If one substituted Robertson with a Taliban cleric and switched the words "socialist" and "capitalism," the Western political class, the media, and other non-Muslim religious leaders would have a field day attacking the primitive nature of Islam and its radicalism while ignoring the diversity within the Muslim world that consists of billions of people from different cultures, classes, and ethnicities. Hence, institutional mechanisms in the West and in much of the world function, by and large, to contain and maintain these so-called primitive Third World cultures that are often silenced by the incessant speech of the dominant culture so as to make these "silent sections of cultures" invisible or, at least, outside the parameters of public discussion or debate. Engaging Freire's *conscientization* process could help reveal the West's penchant for engaging in the construction of invisibility to keep the submerged cultures invisible and also to hide the West's own extremism, which is no less terroristic than Muslim extremism. How else would we characterize the American savagery in Afghanistan, Iraq, and Vietnam that "often extended to the utmost depravity: gratuitous torture, killing for target practice, slaughter of children and babies"[36]—slaughter that pro-life advocate Pat Robertson and his ilk conveniently refuse to address in ethical and political terms? Our inability or unwillingness to engage a *conscientization* process is why we can easily accept Pat Robertson's blatant lies about feminism even as we embrace the false dichotomy encoded in the distinction between First World and Third World contexts—an ideological distinction that primarily functions to reproduce the Western narrative of Third World "savage and primitive" cultures which, in turn, call for the West to exercise its "moral responsibility" to "slaughter children and babies" in order to save them from themselves—a slaughter justified by an American military superior in the Marines as "tough shit, they grow up to be VC [Vietcong]."[37] Too many Americans also remain silent when "drones" and "smart bombs" kill women and children indiscriminately in Afghanistan and Pakistan while the United States presents itself as an advocate for women's rights and freedoms. Western media, political pundits, and most academics also remain silent with respect to the West's extremism as revealed in "the classic former Secretary of State Madeleine Albright's response of 1996 to the reported 500,000 Iraqi children—casualties of 'the sanctions of mass destruction'—'it was worth it.'"[38]

The social construction of not seeing with respect to the United States foreign policy is not all that different from the phenomenon of some academics and researchers who are busily writing grant proposals to study and promote, for example, literacy in Haiti while ignoring the tens of thousands of Haitians in the United States who are struggling and dropping out of the public schools that often surround their universities. The devastating 2010 earthquake in Haiti and the subsequent cholera epidemic that was brought by the United Nations troops has put Haiti on the radar of Western countries whose response has exemplified a kind of paternalism turned into charitable racism, which, according to Albert Memmi, is "a consubstantial part of colonialism."[39] White academics and researchers go to Haiti to collect data and anthropologize the suffering Haitians who are the subjects of their study, returning to their US campuses to tell exotic stories to their students and colleagues, publish their research studies, and obtain tenure, while tens of thousands of Haitians remain in Haiti sentenced to slum conditions and making cookies out of mud to trick their stomachs that they are full and therefore not hungry. Further, these anthropological tourists that go to Haiti to study Haitians and collect data, often discriminate against Haitian students who take their classes in the United States. I remember asking a white American professor who often went to Haiti as part of research projects sponsored by federal grants in the 1980s why he did not devote some of his time working with the thousands of Haitians who surrounded his university. His response was honest if not pathetic: "The funding agencies do not find Haitians in the U.S. 'sexy' enough." Had this liberal First World academic engaged in an honest and rigorous *conscientization* process, he would probably not have remained so comfortable making a career off the trials of millions of Haitians who remain chained to inhumanity, savage inequality, and human misery. Had he been able to make a linkage between his careerist goals and the reproduction of oppression in Haiti largely supported by US foreign policy, he would probably have detected the pathology of his honest answer. This researcher might have developed a deeper comprehension of Haitians and understood that their current life conditions had been shaped, in large part, by American interventionist policies through invasions of Haiti, its occupation, and the perpetual support for right-wing dictators who work largely against the interests of the vast majority of Haitians. By engaging in a form of honest reflection and self-interrogation, the white American researcher would possibly have realized that his political project is, first and foremost, the advancement of his career. Had this First World academic made these linkages, he would likely have denounced the almost sainthood status bestowed upon former president Clinton and former president Bush Sr for their humanitarian work in Haiti after the deadly earthquake. This white American educator might have come to see that both former presidents were partly responsible, through their foreign policies, for the sea of human misery that predated the earthquake. What the earthquake did was both exacerbate the sub-human conditions to which tens of thousands of Haitians were relegated and make them public in the same manner that Hurricane Katrina exposed the structural racism and dehumanization of African Americans in New Orleans. Notwithstanding the horror of the Haitian earthquake, the First World liberal educator would probably refuse to pay $1,320 a night per room in a luxury "five-star" Royal hotel overlooking the shanty towns, shacks, and tents, and which was constructed with "$7.5 million from the World Bank's International Finance Corporation . . . and $2 million from the Clinton Bush Haiti Fund."[40] While this obscene display of First World opulence, if not decadence, marked the humanitarian generosity of First World countries, over one million Haitians displaced by the earthquake remain homeless and continue to exist in sub-human conditions, living in shacks and tents without plumbing or running water, without electricity, and without much to feed themselves and their families. Had the First World educator engaged in the process of *conscientization*, he would possibly be able to detect the false piety demonstrated by former presidents Bush and Clinton as they were greeted by thousands of Haitians in Port-au-Prince. Former president Bush's condescending disdain for Haitian people became quite evident on YouTube all over the world when he tried to wipe his hand, after shaking it with a Haitian man in the crowd, on former president Clinton's shirt.

The *conscientization* process might have lifted the veil of privilege that the *blans*[41] enjoy in Haiti. These are the white or outsiders/ foreigners who fall in love with the exotic narrative of Haiti they create to fulfill their colonial desires and meet their own needs—a narrative that has, in many respects, little to do with the reality that Haitians experience on a daily basis as they try to survive. In many ways, these First World *blans,* regardless of their political orientation, fail to understand how their brand of intervention is nothing like Freire's

pedagogy of the oppressed, [which is] animated by authentic, humanist (not humanitarian) generosity [that] presents itself as a pedagogy of humankind. Pedagogy which begins with the egoistic interests of the oppressors (an egoism cloaked in the false generosity of paternalism) and makes the oppressed the objects of its humanitarianism, itself maintains and embodies oppression. It is an instrument of dehumanization.[42]

Humanitarianism as the embodiment of dehumanization is best exemplified by the Red Cross, a charitable organization which collected over $400 million to alleviate the suffering of tens of thousands of Haitians displaced and made homeless by the earthquake and has as its signature the building of a luxury hotel costing millions of dollars[43] while over one million Haitians remain homeless. While lavish hotels can provide stress relief for the army of NGOs and other humanitarian help as they celebrate "happy hour" with other *blan* friends and co-workers who command First World salaries, tens of thousands of Haitians continue to struggle to put a roof over their heads and scavenge enough to eat so they can reclaim their "ontological and historical vocation to be more fully human."[44] While foreign workers maintain the material conditions to access five-star restaurants and health care services, including psychological therapy, most Haitians displaced by the 2010 earthquake yearn to know what it means to be fully human. Take, for example, Amy Wilentz's

> characterization of Mac McClelland, a human rights reporter for *Mother Jones* who acquired PTSD like it was a cold virus by watching a recently raped Haitian woman collapse at a chance of sighting her attacker. Thus traumatized, McClelland published an account of the home therapy she elected: arranging for a friend to rape her, with the maximum verisimilitude their relationship would allow.[45]

While McClelland's choice of therapy for the exposure to violence in her humanitarian work in the aftermath of the earthquake in Haiti smacks of narcissism on steroids, in varying degrees it also represents the embedded "egoism cloaked in the false generosity of paternalism" of the oppressors' humanitarian interventions packaged as charitable gifts which, in turn, encapsulate the self-centered benevolence of the First World order. These charitable interventions have not only been, for the most part, huge failures (as in the case of Haiti), but First World humanitarians fail to understand that liberation comes only through a process of resolution of tensions and contradictions in the relation between the oppressor and the oppressed. Hence "if the goal of the oppressed is to become fully human, they do not achieve their goal by merely reversing the terms of the contradiction, by changing poles."[46] By the same token, the oppressor cannot expect to liberate the oppressed by reversing the poles so as to experience directly the violence of oppression. This is the continuation of the oppressor's need to appropriate even the oppressed's suffering, as McClelland's case seems to indicate. McClelland's choice of therapy is tantamount to the phenomenon of many liberal educators who feel that they need to make a public statement regarding their divestment from the "dominating bureaucracy"[47] from which they have always reaped benefits, by moving their families into the ghettos temporarily until their own kids have to go to school. According to Freire, liberation is never about the democratization of violence, human misery, and obscene poverty. Liberation that resolves the contradictions between the oppressor and the oppressed can only do so "by the appearance of the new man [and woman]: neither oppressor nor oppressed, but man [and woman] in the process of liberation."[48]

The inability to resolve the contradictions between the oppressor and the oppressed, to make linkages, and to become a "tramp of the obvious," as Freire would say, is directly related to what Freire identified in *Pedagogy of the Oppressed* as the failings of a prevalent "banking" model of education—a process through which

> education thus becomes an act of depositing, in which the students are the depositories and the teacher is the depositor. Instead of communicating, the teacher issues communiqués and makes deposits which the students patiently receive, memorize, and repeat. This is the "banking" concept of education, in which

the scope of action allowed to the students extends only as far as receiving, filling, and storing the deposits.[49]

The "banking" model of education is largely at work in instrumental literacy programs for the poor, in the form of a competency-based, skills-banking approach to schooling, and even through higher education (the highest form of instrumental literacy for the rich), acquired in the form of professional specialization. However, despite their apparent differences, the two approaches share one common feature: they both prevent the development of critical thinking that enables one to "read the world" critically and to understand the reasons and linkages behind mere facts and behind what may appear seemingly obvious but remains ill understood. Literacy for the poor through the "banking" concept of education is, by and large, characterized by mindless, meaningless drills and exercises given "in preparation for multiple choice exams and writing gobbledygook in imitation of the psycho-babble that surrounds them."[50] This "banking" and instrumental approach to education sets the stage for the anesthetization of the mind, as poet John Ashbery eloquently captures in "What Is Poetry?":

> In school
> All the thoughts got combed out:
> What was left was like a field."[51]

The educational "comb," for those teachers who have uncritically accepted the "banking" model of education, is embodied in practice sheets and workbooks, in mindless computer drills and practices that mark and control the pace of routinization. This drill-and-practice assembly line, numbing the student's capacity for thought, leaves the ground prepared for the teacher's instruction where the

> narration (with the teacher as narrator) leads the students to memorize mechanically the narrated content. Worse yet, it turns them into "containers," into "receptacles" to be filled by the teacher. The more meekly the receptacles permit themselves to be filled, the better students they are[52]

The students then are measured by high-stakes tests that reflect an often militaristic, controlled transaction of the teacher's narration and students' memorization of the mechanically narrated "content." Hence, the dominant effects of this mechanistic "banking" education inevitably create educational structures that favor rote learning and necessarily reduce the priorities of education to the pragmatic requirements of capital, anesthetizing students' critical abilities in order to "domesticate social order for its self-preservation."[53]

At the other end of the spectrum, the domestication of the social order is achieved by an equally mechanistic approach to education for the rich via the hyperspecialization that, on the one hand, deposits high-level skills and, on the other, discourages the linkages of different bodies of knowledge in the name of "pure" and specialized science that produces a specialist subject who, according to the Spanish philosopher José Ortega y Gasset, "knows very well his own tiny corner of the universe [but] is radically ignorant of all the rest."[54] In fact, this inability to make linkages between different bodies of knowledge often produces a level of arrogance exemplified by a math professor in a major university when she stated that she has the right of not knowing. This statement was made in reference to the news coverage of the Iraq War when—perhaps because she was feeling uncomfortable with her colleagues' open opposition to the war—she abruptly proclaimed: "I have a right not to know the news." While she has the *right* to choose not to know, as an academic and citizen in a democratic society she has the *responsibility* of knowing what her leaders are doing—and might better choose to know when human rights are being threatened, for example, by policies full of barbarism, policies that enable horrors like the drone-guided bombing of targets that invariably include the carnage of innocent civilians, women, and children, which policy makers consider an "unfortunate part of war" or simply "collateral damage." The authoritarian insensitivity and total disrespect for human life was again on display when the Philippine president Rodrigo Duterte "instructed the navy and the coast guard that 'if there are kidnappers and they are trying to escape, bomb them all . . . They say "hostage." Sorry, collateral damage."[55]

The social organization of knowledge via rigidly defined disciplinary boundaries further contributes to the formation of the specialist class, that is, engineers, doctors, professors, and so on, with each profession subdivided into more constricted areas of focus. This sort of specialist is "only acquainted with one science, and even of that one only knows the small corner in which he is an active investigator. He even proclaims it as a virtue that he takes no cognizance of what lies outside the narrow territory specially cultivated by himself, and gives the name 'dilettantism' to any curiosity for the general scheme of knowledge."[56] This "dilettantism" is discouraged through the mythical need to discover absolute objective truth within one's narrow specialization and, in the process, it domesticates a form of specialized knowledge that not only produces a rupture with philosophies of social and cultural relations—that foregrounds a plurality of culturally embedded perspectives and knowledges—but also hides behind an ideology that creates and sustains false dichotomies, rigidly delineated by disciplinary boundaries. This ideology also informs the view that "hard science," "objectivity," and "scientific rigor" must be disarticulated from the messy data of "soft science" and from the social and political practices that generate these categories in the first place. In addition, this "banking" model of education produces a fragmentation of knowledge that invariably diminishes the students' critical awareness in favor of accepting reality as a given, and as a consequence undermines the "critical consciousness which would result from their intervention in the world as transformers of that world. The more completely they accept the passive role imposed on them, the more they tend simply to adapt to the world as it is and to the fragmented view of reality deposited in them."[57] The dire result is that occupiers of the most privileged class, with the greatest wealth and opportunity, thus renounce their ontological vocation as agents of history who might not only transform their world but also reflect on that transformation.

According to Freire, "the capability of banking education to minimize or annul the students' creative power and to stimulate their credulity serves the interest of the oppressors, who care neither to have the world revealed nor see it transformed."[58]

The "banking" model of education is also often used as a safe haven for most conservative and many liberal educators who conceal their materialist and consumerist conception of education in what Freire calls a "'digestive' concept of knowledge, so common in current educational practice"[59]—a practice that considers students to be "undernourished" and, as a result, leads the teacher to feel compelled to give students an unrealistic list of readings that are never really covered or discussed in class under the pretext that the students' "consciousness is 'spatialized,' and must be 'filled' in order to know."[60] I am reminded of a professor who gave his student a syllabus containing a reading list totaling 80 pages, knowing all too well that it is impossible to rigorously discuss all of these readings in a one-semester course, a pedagogy that certainly celebrates quantity over quality. The same professor required students to write a 40-page paper (why not 25, 35, or 38?)—pages that he hardly read much less provided extensive and insightful comments. In a student's corrected 54-page paper, the professor provided short comments that did not go beyond 2 to 5 words such as "excellent job," "high vs. low culture," "great," or "pedagogical forces." In short, an entire 54-page paper received a total of 43 words in comments. This "nutritionist" approach to education follows the "same conception [that] led Jean Paul Sartre, [when] criticizing the notion that 'to know is to eat,' to exclaim: 'O philosophie alimentaire!'"[61]—a process where "words are transformed into mere 'deposit of vocabulary' [the teacher's vocabulary]—the bread of the spirit which the [students] are to 'eat' and 'digest'"[62] the teacher's knowledge (i.e., definition lists without the apprehension of the object of knowledge; methods as a tool kit divorced from awareness of how their use inscribes certain ideologies, particularly now as applied to new technologies;

formulaic texts masquerading as theory that belittles practice; and ample glossaries). Incessantly "fed" information as unthinking receptacles, students are later asked to "vomit" it back in the mandated exams and tests designed, on the one hand, to confirm the teacher's superior knowledge/bank-account and, on the other, to feed his or her narcissistic needs, a motive inherent in most humanitarian (not humanist) approaches to education. In the end, the "nutritionist banking" approach to education, even when offered under the guise of progressive education, has as its major goal the fattening of the student's brain through the "deposits" of the teacher's knowledge and thus, under this pedagogical model, students absorb understandings "not born of [their own] . . . creative efforts . . . [as] learners."[63] This kind of education, concerned with the reproduction of facts rather than apprehending the object of knowledge in order to produce new knowledge, invariably results in the paralysis of the learner's epistemological curiosity and creativity due to the overload of the teacher's imposed knowledge, "which in fact [is] . . . almost completely alienating and alienated, having so little, if anything, to do with the student's socio-cultural reality."[64]

In essence, in *Pedagogy of the Oppressed*, Freire offers us an ideological road map for revolutionary transformations based on praxis where there is "no dichotomy by which this praxis could be divided into a prior stage of reflection and a subsequent stage. Action and reflection occur simultaneously."[65] Simply put, Freire challenges all of us to develop critical reflective tools that will keep us from forgetting dangerous memories which are marked by draconian economic inequality, cruel violence, and dehumanization—a dehumanization that needs to be denounced. This condemnation of human suffering must happen so that we can protect the intellectual coherence needed in order to help others comprehend the critical difference between studying hunger as anthropological tourists and experiencing it, between deploring violence and surviving it, and between the false benevolence of "giving voice" and being institutionally forced into voicelessness. Thus, the pseudo-critical educators who proclaim the need to "give" people of color or women a voice, fail to realize that voice is not a gift. It is a democratic right. It is a human right.

Freire always emphasized that the raison d'etre of struggles for liberation is the reclamation of these rights, which can never be achieved without autonomy. In turn, autonomy cannot be achieved without a true communion with the people with whom we are engaged in a struggle for liberation. In other words, the dominant language of critique that denounces social injustices through written discursive practice only, but which lacks a corresponding action together with the people, represents a situational communion. This is often the case when academics, as anthropological tourists, enter into communion with the people for a brief time while, for example, collecting data for their research project, but leave the struggling community at its own mercy soon after. Communion with the oppressed means one's willingness to commit class and race suicide which represents much more than "the mere crossing border from one space to another geographical crossing from oppressor to oppressed . . . . Class suicide is a form of Easter; it involves problematizing a passage through a cultural and ideological context. It is the commitment to meaningful and lasting solidarity with the oppressed that counts."[66] As Freire succinctly put it,

> denial of communion in the revolutionary process, avoidance of dialogue with people under the pretext of organizing them, of strengthening revolutionary power, or ensuring a united front, is really a fear of freedom. It is fear of lack of faith in the people . . . [t]he revolution is made neither by the leaders for the people, nor by the people for the leaders, but by both acting together in unshakable solidarity. This solidarity is born only when the leaders witness to it by their humble, loving, and courageous encounter with the people. Not all men and women have sufficient courage for this encounter—but when they avoid encounter they become inflexible and treat others

as mere objects; instead of nurturing life, they kill life; instead of searching for life, they flee from it. And these are oppressor characteristics.[67]

# References

1  Vivianne Rodrigues, "New York's $25,000 Dessert Sets Guinness Record," *Reuters* (November 7, 2007), http://www.reuters.com/article/us-dessert-idUSN0753679220071107.
2  Paulo Freire, *Pedagogy of the Oppressed* (New York: Continuum, 1970), p. 67.
3  *Ibid.*
4  *Ibid.*, p. 66.
5  *Ibid.*
6  Stanley Aronowitz, "Forward," *Critical Pedagogy in Uncertain Times: Hope and Possibilities*, ed. Sheila L. Macrine (New York: Palgrave MacMillan, 2009), p. ix.
7  Paulo Freire and Donaldo Macedo, "A Dialogue, Language, and Race," *Harvard Educational Review*, vol. 65, no. 3 (Fall 1995), pp. 377–402.
8  Paulo Freire, *Letters to Cristina: Reflections on My Life and Work* (New York: Routledge, 1966), p. 21.
9  *Ibid.*
10  Henry A. Giroux, "Radical Pedagogy and Educated Hope: Remembering Paulo Freire." Typewritten manuscript.
11  *Ibid.*
12  Paulo Freire and Donaldo Macedo, Typewritten manuscript.
13  Freire, *Letters to Cristina*, p. 23.
14  *Ibid.*, p. 41.
15  *Ibid.*, p. 24.
16  *Ibid.*, p. 15.
17  Ana Maria Araújo Freire, "Prologue" in *Pedagogy of Indignation* (Boulder, CO: Paradigm Publishers, 2004), p. xxvii.
18  *Ibid.*, p. xxvii.
19  https://www.youtube.com/watch?v=2Ll6M0cXV54.
20  *Ibid.*
21  Lilia I. Bartolomé, *Harvard Educational Review*, vol. 64, no. 2 (Summer 1994), pp. 173–94.
22  Paulo Freire, *The Politics of Education: Culture, Power, and Liberation* (New York: Bergin & Garvey, 1985), p. 185.
23  Paulo Freire, *Cultural Action for Freedom* (Cambridge, MA: Harvard Educational Review, 1970), p. 4.
24  *Ibid.*, p. 4.

25   Henry Giroux, "The New Extremism and Politics of Distraction in the Age of Austerity," *Truthout*, January 22, 2013, http://truth-out.org/opinion/item/13998-the-new-extremism-and-politics-of-distraction-in-the-age-of-austerity.

26   Arundhati Roy, "What Have We Done to Democracy?" *The Huffington Post*, September 27, 2009, http://www.huffingtonpost.com/arundhati-roy/what-have-we-done-to-demo_b_301294.html.

27   Tom Horne, interview by Allison Keyes, *Tell Me More*, National Public Radio News, May 13, 2010, http://www.npr.org/templates/story/story.php?storyId=126797959.

28   Arundhati Roy, "What Have We Done to Democracy?"

29   Freire, *Pedagogy of the Oppressed*, p. 85.

30   *Ibid.*

31   *Ibid.* 35. Freire, *The Politics of Education*, p. 172.

32   *Ibid.*, p. 172.

33   *Ibid.*, p. 171.

34   *Ibid.*, p. 172.

35   "Timeless Whoppers—Pat Robertson," *The Nation*, January 10, 2013, http://www.thenation.com/timeless-whoppers-pat-robertson.

36   Jonathan Schell, "The Real American War in Vietnam," *The Nation*, February 4, 2013, http://www.thenation.com/article/172264/real-american-war-vietnam.

37   *Ibid.*

38   Edward S. Herman, "Beyond Chutzpah," *Z Magazine*, February 2013, p. 6.

39   Albert Memmi, *The Colonizer and the Colonized* (Boston: Beacon, 1991).

40   Amy Wilentz, "Letter from Haiti," *The Nation*, January 28, 2013, p. 22.

41   *Ibid.*

42   Freire, *Pedagogy of the Oppressed*, p. 54.

43   Wilentz, "Letter from Haiti," p. 22.

44   Freire, *Pedagogy of the Oppressed*, p. 55.

45   Madison Smartt Bell, "Nine Years in One Day: On Haiti," *The Nation*, January 28, 2013, p. 22.

46   Freire, *Pedagogy of the Oppressed*, p. 56.

47   *Ibid.*, p. 57.

48   *Ibid.*, p. 56.

49   *Ibid.*, p. 72.

50   Patrick L. Courts, *Literacies and Empowerment: The Meaning Makers* (South Hadley, Massachusetts: Bergin & Garvey, 1991), p. 4.

51   John Ashbery, "What Is Poetry," *Houseboat Days: Poems by John Ashbery* (New York: Penguin Books, 1977), p. 47.

52   Freire, *Pedagogy of the Oppressed*, p. 72.

53   Freire, *The Politics of Education*, p. 116.

54   José Ortega y Gasset, *The Revolt of the Masses* (New York: W. W. Norton, 1964), p. 111.

55   "Duterte vows to hit militants, captives," The Boston Globe, January 16, 2017, p. A3.

56   José Ortega y Gasset, *The Revolt of the Masses* (New York: W. W. Norton, 1964), p. 111.

57 Freire, *Pedagogy of the Oppressed*, p. 73.
58 *Ibid.*
59 Paulo Freire, *Cultural Action for Freedom* (Cambridge, MA: Harvard Educational Review, 1970), p. 7.
60 *Ibid.*
61 Cited in Freire, *Cultural Action for Freedom*, p. 8.
62 *Ibid.*
63 *Ibid.*
64 *Ibid.*
65 *Ibid.*, p. 128.
66 Paulo Freire (ed.) with James Fraser, Donaldo Macedo, Tanya McKinnon, and William Stokes, *Mentoring the Mentor: A Critical Dialogue with Paulo Freire* (New York: Peter Lang Publishing, 1997), p. 316.
67 Paulo Freire, *Pedagogy of the Oppressed* (New York: Continuum International Publishing Group, 2000), p. 129.

# Preface

These pages, which introduce *Pedagogy of the Oppressed*, result from my observations during six years of political exile, observations which have enriched those previously afforded by my educational activities in Brazil.

I have encountered, both in training courses which analyze the role of *conscientização*[1] and in actual experimentation with a truly liberating education, the "fear of freedom" discussed in the first chapter of this book. Not infrequently, training course participants call attention to "the danger of *conscientização*" in a way that reveals their own fear of freedom. Critical consciousness, they say, is anarchic. Others add that critical consciousness may lead to disorder. Some, however, confess: Why deny it? I was afraid of freedom. I am no longer afraid!

In one of these discussions, the group was debating whether the *conscientização* of men and women to a specific situation of injustice might not lead them to "destructive fanaticism" or to a "sensation of total collapse of their world." In the midst of the argument, a person who previously had been a factory worker for many years spoke out: "Perhaps I am the only one here of working-class origin. I can't say that I've understood everything you've said just now, but I can say one thing—when I began this course I was *naïve*, and when I found out how naïve I was, I started to get *critical*. But this discovery hasn't made me a fanatic, and I don't feel any collapse either."

---

[1] The term *conscientização* refers to learning to perceive social, political, and economic contradictions, and to take action against the oppressive elements of reality. See chapter 3.—Translator's note.

Doubt regarding the possible effects of *conscientização* implies a premise which the doubter does not always make explicit: It is better for the victims of injustice not to recognize themselves as such. In fact, however, *conscientização* does not lead people to "destructive fanaticism." On the contrary, by making it possible for people to enter the historical process as responsible Subjects,[2] *conscientização* enrolls them in the search for self-affirmation and thus avoids fanaticism.

> The awakening of critical consciousness leads the way to the expression of social discontents precisely because these discontents are real components of an oppressive situation.[3]

Fear of freedom, of which its possessor is not necessarily aware, makes him see ghosts. Such an individual is actually taking refuge in an attempt to achieve security, which he or she prefers to the risks of liberty. As Hegel testifies:

> It is solely by risking life that freedom is obtained; . . . the individual who has not staked his or her life may, no doubt, be recognized as a Person; but he or she has not attained the truth of this recognition as an independent self-consciousness.[4]

Men and women rarely admit their fear of freedom openly, however, tending rather to camouflage it—sometimes unconsciously—by presenting themselves as defenders of freedom. They give their doubts and misgivings an air of profound sobriety, as befitting custodians of freedom. But they confuse freedom with the maintenance of the status quo; so that if *conscientização* threatens to place that status quo in question, it thereby seems to constitute a threat to freedom itself.

---

[2] The term *Subjects* denotes those who know and act, in contrast to *objects*, which are known and acted upon.—Translator's note.

[3] Francisco Weffort, in the preface to Paulo Freire, *Educação como Prática da Liberdade* (Rio de Janeiro, 1967).

[4] Georg Hegel, *The Phenomenology of Mind* (New York, 1967), p. 233.

Thought and study alone did not produce *Pedagogy of the Oppressed;* it is rooted in concrete situations and describes the reactions of laborers (peasant or urban) and of middle-class persons whom I have observed directly or indirectly during the course of my educative work. Continued observation will afford me an opportunity to modify or to corroborate in later studies the points proposed in this introductory work.

This volume will probably arouse negative reactions in a number of readers. Some will regard my position vis-à-vis the problem of human liberation as purely idealistic, or may even consider discussion of ontological vocation, love, dialogue, hope, humility, and sympathy as so much reactionary "blah." Others will not (or will not wish to) accept my denunciation of a state of oppression that gratifies the oppressors. Accordingly, this admittedly tentative work is for radicals. I am certain that Christians and Marxists, though they may disagree with me in part or in whole, will continue reading to the end. But the reader who dogmatically assumes closed, "irrational" positions will reject the dialogue I hope this book will open.

Sectarianism, fed by fanaticism, is always castrating. Radicalization, nourished by a critical spirit, is always creative. Sectarianism mythicizes and thereby alienates; radicalization criticizes and thereby liberates. Radicalization involves increased commitment to the position one has chosen, and thus ever greater engagement in the effort to transform concrete, objective reality. Conversely, sectarianism, because it is mythicizing and irrational, turns reality into a false (and therefore unchangeable) "reality."

Sectarianism in any quarter is an obstacle to the emancipation of mankind. The rightist version thereof does not always, unfortunately, call forth its natural counterpart: radicalization of the revolutionary. Not infrequently, revolutionaries themselves become reactionary by falling into sectarianism in the process of responding to the sectarianism of the Right. This possibility, however, should not lead the radical to become a docile pawn of the elites. Engaged in the process of liberation, he or she cannot remain passive in the face of the oppressor's violence.

On the other hand, the radical is never a subjectivist. For this individual the subjective aspect exists only in relation to the objective aspect (the concrete reality, which is the object of analysis). Subjectivity and objectivity thus join in a dialectical unity producing knowledge in solidarity with action, and vice versa.

For his or her part, the sectarian of whatever persuasion, blinded by irrationality, does not (or cannot) perceive the dynamic of reality—or else misinterprets it. Should this person think dialectically, it is with a "domesticated dialectic." The rightist sectarian (whom I have previously termed a *born sectarian*[5]) wants to slow down the historical process, to "domesticate" time and thus to domesticate men and women. The leftist-turned-sectarian goes totally astray when he or she attempts to interpret reality and history dialectically, and falls into essentially fatalistic positions.

The rightist sectarian differs from his or her leftist counterpart in that the former attempts to domesticate the present so that (he or she hopes) the future will reproduce this domesticated present, while the latter considers the future pre-established—a kind of inevitable fate, fortune, or destiny. For the rightist sectarian, "today," linked to the past, is something given and immutable; for the leftist sectarian, "tomorrow" is decreed beforehand, is inexorably preordained. This rightist and this leftist are both reactionary because, starting from their respectively false views of history, both develop forms of action that negate freedom. The fact that one person imagines a "well-behaved" present and the other a predetermined future does not mean that they therefore fold their arms and become spectators (the former expecting that the present will continue, the latter waiting for the already "known" future to come to pass). On the contrary, closing themselves into "circles of certainty" from which they cannot escape, these individuals "make" their own truth. It is not the truth of men and women who struggle to build the future, running the risks involved in this very construction. Nor is it the truth of men and women who fight side by side and learn together

---

[5] In *Educação como Prática da Liberdade.*

how to build this future—which is not something given to be received by people, but is rather something to be created by them. Both types of sectarian, treating history in an equally proprietary fashion, end up without the people—which is another way of being against them.

Whereas the rightist sectarian, closing himself in "his" truth, does no more than fulfill a natural role, the leftist who becomes sectarian and rigid negates his or her very nature. Each, however, as he revolves about "his" truth, feels threatened if that truth is questioned. Thus, each considers anything that is not "his" truth a lie. As the journalist Marcio Moreira Alves once told me, "They both suffer from an absence of doubt."

The radical, committed to human liberation, does not become the prisoner of a "circle of certainty within which reality is also imprisoned. On the contrary, the more radical the person is, the more fully he or she enters into reality so that, knowing it better, he or she can better transform it. This individual is not afraid to confront, to listen, to see the world unveiled. This person is not afraid to meet the people or to enter into dialogue with them.[6] This person does not consider himself or herself the proprietor of history or of all people, or the liberator of the oppressed; but he or she does commit himself or herself, within history, to fight at their side.

The pedagogy of the oppressed, the introductory outlines of which are presented in the following pages, is a task for radicals; it cannot be carried out by sectarians.

I will be satisfied if among the readers of this work there are those sufficiently critical to correct mistakes and misunderstandings, to deepen affirmations and to point out aspects I have not perceived. It is possible that some may question my right to discuss revolutionary cultural action, a subject of which I have no concrete experience. The fact that I have not personally participated in revolutionary action, however, does not negate the possibility of my reflecting on

---

[6] "As long as theoretic knowledge remains the privilege of a handful of 'academicians in the Party, the latter will face the danger of going astray." Rosa Luxembourg, *Reform or Revolution,* cited in C. Wright Mills, *The Marxists* (New York, 1963).

this theme. Furthermore, in my experience as an educator with the people, using a dialogical and problem-posing education, I have accumulated a comparative wealth of material that challenged me to run the risk of making the affirmations contained in this work.

From these pages I hope at least the following will endure: my trust in the people, and my faith in men and women, and in the creation of a world in which it will be easier to love.

Here I would like to express my gratitude to Elza, my wife and "first reader," for the understanding and encouragement she has shown my work, which belongs to her as well. I would also like to extend my thanks to a group of friends for their comments on my manuscript. At the risk of omitting some names, I must mention João da Veiga Coutinho, Richard Shaull, Jim Lamb, Myra and Jovelino Ramos, Paulo de Tarso, Almino Affonso, Plinio Sampaio, Ernani Maria Fiori, Marcela Gajardo, José Luis Fiori, and João Zacarioti. The responsibility for the affirmations made herein is, of course, mine alone.

PAULO FREIRE

# Pedagogy of the Oppressed

# CHAPTER

# 1

While the problem of humanization has always, from an axiological point of view, been humankind's central problem, it now takes on the character of an inescapable concern.[1] Concern for humanization leads at once to the recognition of dehumanization, not only as an ontological possibility but as an historical reality. And as an individual perceives the extent of dehumanization, he or she may ask if humanization is a viable possibility. Within history, in concrete, objective contexts, both humanization and dehumanization are possibilities for a person as an uncompleted being conscious of their incompletion.

But while both humanization and dehumanization are real alternatives, only the first is the people's vocation. This vocation is constantly negated, yet it is affirmed by that very negation. It is

---

[1] The current movements of rebellion, especially those of youth, while they necessarily reflect the peculiarities of their respective settings, manifest in their essence this preoccupation with people as beings in the world and with the world—preoccupation with *what* and *how* they are "being." As they place consumer civilization in judgment, denounce bureaucracies of all types, demand the transformation of the universities (changing the rigid nature of the teacher-student relationship and placing that relationship within the context of reality), propose the transformation of reality itself so that universities can be renewed, attack old orders and established institutions in the attempt to affirm human beings as the Subjects of decision, all these movements reflect the style of our age, which is more anthropological than anthropocentric.

thwarted by injustice, exploitation, oppression, and the violence of the oppressors; it is affirmed by the yearning of the oppressed for freedom and justice, and by their struggle to recover their lost humanity.

Dehumanization, which marks not only those whose humanity has been stolen, but also (though in a different way) those who have stolen it, is a *distortion* of the vocation of becoming more fully human. This distortion occurs within history; but it is not an historical vocation. Indeed, to admit of dehumanization as an historical vocation would lead either to cynicism or total despair. The struggle for humanization, for the emancipation of labor, for the overcoming of alienation, for the affirmation of men and women as persons would be meaningless. This struggle is possible only because dehumanization, although a concrete historical fact, is *not* a given destiny but the result of an unjust order that engenders violence in the oppressors, which in turn dehumanizes the oppressed.

Because it is a distortion of being more fully human, sooner or later being less human leads the oppressed to struggle against those who made them so. In order for this struggle to have meaning, the oppressed must not, in seeking to regain their humanity (which is a way to create it), become in turn oppressors of the oppressors, but rather restorers of the humanity of both.

This, then, is the great humanistic and historical task of the oppressed: to liberate themselves and their oppressors as well. The oppressors, who oppress, exploit, and rape by virtue of their power, cannot find in this power the strength to liberate either the oppressed or themselves. Only power that springs from the weakness of the oppressed will be sufficiently strong to free both. Any attempt to "soften" the power of the oppressor in deference to the weakness of the oppressed almost always manifests itself in the form of false generosity; indeed, the attempt never goes beyond this. In order to have the continued opportunity to express their "generosity," the oppressors must perpetuate injustice as well. An unjust social order is the permanent fount of this "generosity," which is nourished by death, despair, and poverty. That is why the dispensers of false generosity become desperate at the slightest threat to its source.

True generosity consists precisely in fighting to destroy the causes which nourish false charity. False charity constrains the fearful and subdued, the "rejects of life," to extend their trembling hands. True generosity lies in striving so that these hands—whether of individuals or entire peoples—need be extended less and less in supplication, so that more and more they become human hands which work and, working, transform the world.

This lesson and this apprenticeship must come, however, from the oppressed themselves and from those who are truly solidary with them. As individuals or as peoples, by fighting for the restoration of their humanity they will be attempting the restoration of true generosity. Who are better prepared than the oppressed to understand the terrible significance of an oppressive society? Who suffer the effects of oppression more than the oppressed? Who can better understand the necessity of liberation? They will not gain this liberation by chance but through the praxis of their quest for it, through their recognition of the necessity to fight for it. And this fight, because of the purpose given it by the oppressed, will actually constitute an act of love opposing the lovelessness which lies at the heart of the oppressors' violence, lovelessness even when clothed in false generosity.

But almost always, during the initial stage of the struggle, the oppressed, instead of striving for liberation, tend themselves to become oppressors, or "sub-oppressors." The very structure of their thought has been conditioned by the contradictions of the concrete, existential situation by which they were shaped. Their ideal is to be men; but for them, to be men is to be oppressors. This is their model of humanity. This phenomenon derives from the fact that the oppressed, at a certain moment of their existential experience, adopt an attitude of "adhesion" to the oppressor. Under these circumstances they cannot "consider" him sufficiently clearly to objectivize him—to discover him "outside" themselves. This does not necessarily mean that the oppressed are unaware that they are downtrodden. But their perception of themselves as oppressed is impaired by their submersion in the reality of oppression. At this level, their perception of themselves as opposites of the oppressor does not yet signify engagement in a struggle to overcome the contradiction;[2] the one pole aspires not to liberation, but to identification with its opposite pole.

In this situation the oppressed do not see the "new man" as the person to be born from the resolution of this contradiction, as oppression gives way to liberation. For them, the new man or woman themselves become oppressors. Their vision of the new man or woman is individualistic; because of their identification with the oppressor, they have no consciousness of themselves as persons or as members of an oppressed class. It is not to become free that they want agrarian reform, but in order to acquire land and thus become landowners—or, more precisely, bosses over other workers. It is a rare peasant who, once "promoted" to overseer, does not become more of a tyrant towards his former comrades than the owner himself. This is because the context of the peasant's situation, that is, oppression, remains unchanged. In this example, the overseer, in order to make sure of his job, must be as tough as the owner—and more so. Thus is illustrated our previous assertion that during the initial stage of their struggle the oppressed find in the oppressor their model of "manhood."

Even revolution, which transforms a concrete situation of oppression by establishing the process of liberation, must confront this phenomenon. Many of the oppressed who directly or indirectly participate in revolution intend—conditioned by the myths of the old order—to make it their private revolution. The shadow of their former oppressor is still cast over them.

The "fear of freedom" which afflicts the oppressed,[3] a fear which may equally well lead them to desire the role of oppressor or bind them to the role of oppressed, should be examined. One of the basic elements of the relationship between oppressor and oppressed is

---

[2]   As used throughout this book, the term "contradiction" denotes the dialectical conflict between opposing social forces.—Translator's note.

[3]   This fear of freedom is also to be found in the oppressors, though, obviously, in a different form. The oppressed are afraid to embrace freedom; the oppressors are afraid of losing the "freedom" to oppress.

*prescription.* Every prescription represents the imposition of one individual's choice upon another, transforming the consciousness of the person prescribed to into one that conforms with the prescriber's consciousness. Thus, the behavior of the oppressed is a prescribed behavior, following as it does the guidelines of the oppressor.

The oppressed, having internalized the image of the oppressor and adopted his guidelines, are fearful of freedom. Freedom would require them to eject this image and replace it with autonomy and responsibility. Freedom is acquired by conquest, not by gift. It must be pursued constantly and responsibly. Freedom is not an ideal located outside of man; nor is it an idea which becomes myth. It is rather the indispensable condition for the quest for human completion.

To surmount the situation of oppression, people must first critically recognize its causes, so that through transforming action they can create a new situation, one which makes possible the pursuit of a fuller humanity. But the struggle to be more fully human has already begun in the authentic struggle to transform the situation. Although the situation of oppression is a dehumanized and dehumanizing totality affecting both the oppressors and those whom they oppress, it is the latter who must, from their stifled humanity, wage for both the struggle for a fuller humanity; the oppressor, who is himself dehumanized because he dehumanizes others, is unable to lead this struggle.

However, the oppressed, who have adapted to the structure of domination in which they are immersed, and have become resigned to it, are inhibited from waging the struggle for freedom so long as they feel incapable of running the risks it requires. Moreover, their struggle for freedom threatens not only the oppressor, but also their own oppressed comrades who are fearful of still greater repression. When they discover within themselves the yearning to be free, they perceive that this yearning can be transformed into reality only when the same yearning is aroused in their comrades. But while dominated by the fear of freedom they refuse to appeal to others, or to listen to the appeals of others, or even to the appeals of their own conscience. They prefer gregariousness to authentic comradeship; they prefer the security of conformity with their state of unfreedom to the creative communion produced by freedom and even the very pursuit of freedom.

The oppressed suffer from the duality which has established itself in their innermost being. They discover that without freedom they cannot exist authentically. Yet, although they desire authentic existence, they fear it. They are at one and the same time themselves and the oppressor whose consciousness they have internalized. The conflict lies in the choice between being wholly themselves or being divided; between ejecting the oppressor within or not ejecting them; between human solidarity or alienation; between following prescriptions or having choices; between being spectators or actors; between acting or having the illusion of acting through the action of the oppressors; between speaking out or being silent, castrated in their power to create and re-create, in their power to transform the world. This is the tragic dilemma of the oppressed which their education must take into account.

This book will present some aspects of what the writer has termed the pedagogy of the oppressed, a pedagogy which must be forged *with,* not *for,* the oppressed (whether individuals or peoples) in the incessant struggle to regain their humanity. This pedagogy makes oppression and its causes objects of reflection by the oppressed, and from that reflection will come their necessary engagement in the struggle for their liberation. And in the struggle this pedagogy will be made and remade.

The central problem is this: How can the oppressed, as divided, unauthentic beings, participate in developing the pedagogy of their liberation? Only as they discover themselves to be "hosts" of the oppressor can they contribute to the midwifery of their liberating pedagogy. As long as they live in the duality in which *to be* is *to be like,* and *to be like* is *to be like the oppressor,* this contribution is impossible. The pedagogy of the oppressed is an instrument for their critical discovery that both they and their oppressors are manifestations of dehumanization.

Liberation is thus a childbirth, and a painful one. The man or woman who emerges is a new person, viable only as the oppressor-oppressed contradiction is superseded by the humanization of all people. Or to put it another way, the solution of this contradiction is born in the labor which brings into the world this new being: no longer oppressor nor longer oppressed, but human in the process of achieving freedom.

This solution cannot be achieved in idealistic terms. In order for the oppressed to be able to wage the struggle for their liberation, they must perceive the reality of oppression not as a closed world from which there is no exit, but as a limiting situation which they can transform. This perception is a necessary but not a sufficient condition for liberation; it must become the motivating force for liberating action. Nor does the discovery by the oppressed that they exist in dialectical relationship to the oppressor, as his antithesis—that without them the oppressor could not exist[4]—in itself constitute liberation. The oppressed can overcome the contradiction in which they are caught only when this perception enlists them in the struggle to free themselves.

The same is true with respect to the individual oppressor as a person. Discovering himself to be an oppressor may cause considerable anguish, but it does not necessarily lead to solidarity with the oppressed. Rationalizing his guilt through paternalistic treatment of the oppressed, all the while holding them fast in a position of dependence, will not do. Solidarity requires that one enter into the situation of those with whom one is solidary; it is a radical posture. If what characterizes the oppressed is their subordination to the consciousness of the master, as Hegel affirms,[5] true solidarity with the oppressed means fighting at their side to transform the objective reality which has made them these "beings for another." The oppres-

---

[4] See Hegel, *op. cit.*, pp. 236–237.

[5] Analyzing the dialectical relationship between the consciousness of the master and the consciousness of the oppressed, Hegel states: "The one is independent, and its essential nature is to be for itself; the other is dependent, and its essence is life or existence for another. The former is the Master, or Lord, the latter the Bondsman." *Ibid.*, p. 234.

sor is solidary with the oppressed only when he stops regarding the oppressed as an abstract category and sees them as persons who have been unjustly dealt with, deprived of their voice, cheated in the sale of their labor—when he stops making pious, sentimental, and individualistic gestures and risks an act of love. True solidarity is found only in the plenitude of this act of love, in its existentiality, in its praxis. To affirm that men and women are persons and as persons should be free, and yet to do nothing tangible to make this affirmation a reality, is a farce.

Since it is a concrete situation that the oppressor-oppressed contradiction is established, the resolution of this contradiction must be *objectively* verifiable. Hence, the radical requirement—both for the individual who discovers himself or herself to be an oppressor and for the oppressed—that the concrete situation which begets oppression must be transformed.

To present this radical demand for the objective transformation of reality, to combat subjectivist immobility which would divert the recognition of oppression into patient waiting for oppression to disappear by itself, is not to dismiss the role of subjectivity in the struggle to change structures. On the contrary, one cannot conceive of objectivity without subjectivity. Neither can exist without the other, nor can they be dichotomized. The separation of objectivity from subjectivity, the denial of the latter when analyzing reality or acting upon it, is objectivism. On the other hand, the denial of objectivity in analysis or action, resulting in a subjectivism which leads to solipsistic positions, denies action itself by denying objective reality. Neither objectivism nor subjectivism, nor yet psychologism is propounded here, but rather subjectivity and objectivity in constant dialectical relationship.

To deny the importance of subjectivity in the process of transforming the world and history is naive and simplistic. It is to admit the impossible: a world without people. This objectivistic position is as ingenuous as that of subjectivism, which postulates people without a world. World and human beings do not exist apart from each other, they exist in constant interaction. Marx does not espouse such a dichotomy, nor does any other critical, realistic thinker. What Marx criticized and scientifically destroyed was not subjectivity, but subjectivism and psychologism. Just as objective social reality exists not by chance, but as the product of human action, so it is not transformed by chance. If humankind produce social reality (which in the "inversion of the praxis" turns back upon them and conditions them), then transforming that reality is an historical task, a task for humanity.

Reality which becomes oppressive results in the contradistinction of men as oppressors and oppressed. The latter, whose task it is to struggle for their liberation together with those who show true solidarity, must acquire a critical awareness of oppression through the praxis of this struggle. One of the gravest obstacles to the achievement of liberation is that oppressive reality absorbs those within it and thereby acts to submerge human beings' consiousness.[6] Functionally, oppression is domesticating. To no longer be prey to its force, one must emerge from it and turn upon it. This can be done only by means of the praxis: reflection and action upon the world in order to transform it.

> Hay que hacer al opresión real todavía mas opresiva añadiendo a aquella la *conciéncia* de la opresión haciendo la infamia todavía mas infamante, al pregonarla.[7]

Making "real oppression more oppressive still by adding to it the realization of oppression" corresponds to the dialectical relation between the subjective and the objective. Only in this interdependence is an authentic praxis possible, without which it is impossible

---

[6] "Liberating action necessarily involves a moment of perception and volition. This action both precedes and follows that moment, to which it first acts as a prologue and which it subsequently serves to effect and continue within history. The action of domination, however, does not necessarily imply this dimension; for the structure of domination is maintained by its own mechanical and unconscious functionality." From an unpublished work by José Luiz Fiori, who has kindly granted permission to quote him.

[7] Karl Marx and Friedrich Engels, *La Sagrada Familia y otros Escritos* (Mexico, 1962), p. 6. Emphasis added.

to resolve the oppressor-oppressed contradiction. To achieve this goal, the oppressed must confront reality critically, simultaneously objectifying and acting upon that reality. A mere perception of reality not followed by this critical intervention will not lead to a transformation of objective reality—precisely because it is not a true perception. This is the case of a purely subjectivist perception by someone who forsakes objective reality and creates a false substitute.

A different type of false perception occurs when a change in objective reality would threaten the individual or class interests of the perceiver. In the first instance, there is no critical intervention in reality because that reality is fictitious; there is none in the second instance because intervention would contradict the class interests of the perceiver. In the latter case the tendency of the perceiver is to behave "neurotically." The fact exists; but both the fact and what may result from it may be prejudicial to the person. Thus it becomes necessary, not precisely to deny the fact, but to "see it differently." This rationalization as a defense mechanism coincides in the end with subjectivism. A fact which is not denied but whose truths are rationalized loses its objective base. It ceases to be concrete and becomes a myth created in defense of the class of the perceiver.

Herein lies one of the reasons for the prohibitions and the difficulties (to be discussed at length in Chapter 4) designed to dissuade the people from critical intervention in reality. The oppressor knows full well that this intervention would not be to his interest. What is to his interest is for the people to continue in a state of submersion, impotent in the face of oppressive reality. Of relevance here is Lukács' warning to the revolutionary party:

> . . . il doit, pour employer les mots de Marx, expliquer aux masses leur propre action non seulement afin d'assurer la continuité des expériences révolutionnaires du prolétariat, mais aussi d'activer consciemment le développement ultérieur de ces expériences.[8]

In affirming this necessity, Lukács is unquestionably posing the

---

[8]  Georg Lukács, *Lénine* (Paris, 1965), p. 62.

problem of critical intervention. "To explain to the masses their own action" is to clarify and illuminate that action, both regarding its relationship to the objective facts by which it was prompted, and regarding its purposes. The more the people unveil this challenging reality which is to be the object of their transforming action, the more critically they enter that reality. In this way they are "consciously activating the subsequent development of their experiences." There would be no human action if there were no objective reality, no world to be the "not I" of the person and to challenge them; just as there would be no human action if humankind were not a "project," if he or she were not able to transcend himself or herself, if one were not able to perceive reality and understand it in order to transform it.

In dialectical thought, world and action are intimately interdependent. But action is human only when it is not merely an occupation but also a preoccupation, that is, when it is not dichotomized from reflection. Reflection, which is essential to action, is implicit in Lukács' requirement of "explaining to the masses their own action," just as it is implicit in the purpose he attributes to this explanation: that of "consciously activating the subsequent development of experience."

For us, however, the requirement is seen not in terms of explaining to, but rather dialoguing with the people about their actions. In any event, no reality transforms itself,[9] and the duty which Lukács ascribes to the revolutionary party of "explaining to the masses their own action" coincides with our affirmation of the need for the critical intervention of the people in reality through the praxis. The pedagogy of the oppressed, which is the pedagogy of people engaged in the fight for their own liberation, has its roots here. And those who recognize, or begin to recognize, themselves

---

[9] "The materialist doctrine that men are products of circumstances and upbringing, and that, therefore, changed men are products of other circumstances and changed upbringing, forgets that it is men that change circumstances and that the educator himself needs educating." Karl Marx and Friedrich Engels, *Selected Works* (New York, 1968), p. 28.

as oppressed must be among the developers of this pedagogy. No pedagogy which is truly liberating can remain distant from the oppressed by treating them as unfortunates and by presenting for their emulation models from among the oppressors. The oppressed must be their own example in the struggle for their redemption.

The pedagogy of the oppressed, animated by authentic, humanist (not humanitarian) generosity, presents itself as a pedagogy of humankind. Pedagogy which begins with the egoistic interests of the oppressors (an egoism cloaked in the false generosity of paternalism) and makes of the oppressed the objects of its humanitarianism, itself maintains and embodies oppression. It is an instrument of dehumanization. This is why, as we affirmed earlier, the pedagogy of the oppressed cannot be developed or practiced by the oppressors. It would be a contradiction in terms if the oppressors not only defended but actually implemented a liberating education.

But if the implementation of a liberating education requires political power and the oppressed have none, how then is it possible to carry out the pedagogy of the oppressed prior to the revolution? This is a question of the greatest importance, the reply to which is at least tentatively outlined in Chapter 4. One aspect of the reply is to be found in the distinction between *systematic education,* which can only be changed by political power, and *educational projects,* which should be carried out *with* the oppressed in the process of organizing them.

The pedagogy of the oppressed, as a humanist and libertarian pedagogy, has two distinct stages. In the first, the oppressed unveil the world of oppression and through the praxis commit themselves to its transformation. In the second stage, in which the reality of oppression has already been transformed, this pedagogy ceases to belong to the oppressed and becomes a pedagogy of all people in the process of permanent liberation. In both stages, it is always through action in depth that the culture of domination is culturally confronted.[10] In the first stage this confrontation occurs through the

---

[10] This appears to be the fundamental aspect of Mao's Cultural Revolution.

change in the way the oppressed perceive the world of oppression; in the second stage, through the expulsion of the myths created and developed in the old order, which like specters haunt the new structure emerging from the revolutionary transformation.

The pedagogy of the first stage must deal with the problem of the oppressed consciousness and the oppressor consciousness, the problem of men and women who oppress and men and women who suffer oppression. It must take into account their behavior, their view of the world, and their ethics. A particular problem is the duality of the oppressed: they are contradictory, divided beings, shaped by and existing in a concrete situation of oppression and violence.

Any situation in which "A" objectively exploits "B" or hinders his and her pursuit of self-affirmation as a responsible person is one of oppression. Such a situation in itself constitutes violence, even when sweetened by false generosity, because it interferes with the individual's ontological and historical vocation to be more fully human. With the establishment of a relationship of oppression, violence has *already* begun. Never in history has violence been initiated by the oppressed. How could they be the initiators, if they themselves are the result of violence? How could they be the sponsors of something whose objective inauguration called forth their existence as oppressed? There would be no oppressed had there been no prior situation of violence to establish their subjugation.

Violence is initiated by those who oppress, who exploit, who fail to recognize others as persons—not by those who are oppressed, exploited, and unrecognized. It is not the unloved who initiate disaffection, but those who cannot love because they love only themselves. It is not the helpless, subject to terror, who initiate terror, but the violent, who with their power create the concrete situation which begets the "rejects of life." It is not the tyrannized who initiate despotism, but the tyrants. It is not the despised who initiate hatred, but those who despise. It is not those whose humanity is denied them who negate humankind, but those who denied that humanity (thus negating their own as well). Force is used not by those who have become weak under the preponderance of the strong, but by the strong who have emasculated them.

For the oppressors, however, it is always the oppressed (whom they obviously never call "the oppressed" but—depending on whether they are fellow countrymen or not—"those people" or "the blind and envious masses" or "savages" or "natives" or "subversives") who are disaffected, who are "violent," "barbaric," "wicked," or "ferocious" when they react to the violence of the oppressors.

Yet it is—paradoxical though it may seem—precisely in the response of the oppressed to the violence of their oppressors that a gesture of love may be found. Consciously or unconsciously, the act of rebellion by the oppressed (an act which is always, or nearly always, as violent as the initial violence of the oppressors) can initiate love. Whereas the violence of the oppressors prevents the oppressed from being fully human, the response of the latter to this violence is grounded in the desire to pursue the right to be human. As the oppressors dehumanize others and violate their rights, they themselves also become dehumanized. As the oppressed, fighting to be human, take away the oppressors' power to dominate and suppress, they restore to the oppressors the humanity they had lost in the exercise of oppression.

It is only the oppressed who, by freeing themselves, can free their oppressors. The latter, as an oppressive class, can free neither others nor themselves. It is therefore essential that the oppressed wage the struggle to resolve the contradiction in which they are caught; and the contradiction will be resolved by the appearance of the new man: neither oppressor nor oppressed, but man in the process of liberation. If the goal of the oppressed is to become fully human, they will not achieve their goal by merely reversing the terms of the contradiction, by simply changing poles.

This may seem simplistic; it is not. Resolution of the oppressor-oppressed contradiction indeed implies the disappearance of the oppressors as a dominant class. However, the restraints imposed by the former oppressed on their oppressors, so that the latter cannot reassume their former position, do not constitute *oppression.* An act is oppressive only when it prevents people from being more fully human. Accordingly, these necessary restraints do not *in themselves* signify that yesterday's oppressed have become today's oppressors. Acts which prevent the restoration of the oppressive regime cannot be compared with those which create and maintain it, cannot be compared with those by which a few men and women deny the majority their right to be human.

However, the moment the new regime hardens into a dominating "bureaucracy"[11] the humanist dimension of the struggle is lost and it is no longer possible to speak of liberation. Hence our insistence that the authentic solution of the oppressor-oppressed contradiction does not lie in a mere reversal of position, in moving from one pole to the other. Nor does it lie in the replacement of the former oppressors with new ones who continue to subjugate the oppressed—all in the name of their liberation.

But even when the contradiction is resolved authentically by a new situation established by the liberated laborers, the former oppressors do not feel liberated. On the contrary, they genuinely consider themselves to be oppressed. Conditioned by the experience of oppressing others, any situation other than their former seems to them like oppression. Formerly, they could eat, dress, wear shoes, be educated, travel, and hear Beethoven; while millions did not eat, had no clothes or shoes, neither studied nor traveled, much less listened to Beethoven. Any restriction on this way of life, in the name of the rights of the community, appears to the former oppressors as a profound violation of their individual rights—although they had no respect for the millions who suffered and died of hunger, pain, sorrow, and despair. For the oppressors, "human beings" refers only to themselves; other people are "things." For the oppressors, there exists only one right: their right to live in peace, over against

---

[11] This rigidity should not be identified with the restraints that must be imposed on the former oppressors so they cannot restore the oppressive order. Rather, it refers to the revolution which becomes stagnant and turns against the people, using the old repressive, bureaucratic State apparatus (which should have been drastically suppressed, as Marx so often emphasized).

the right, not always even recognized, but simply conceded, of the oppressed to survival. And they make this concession only because the existence of the oppressed is necessary to their own existence.

This behavior, this way of understanding the world and people (which necessarily makes the oppressors resist the installation of a new regime) is explained by their experience as a dominant class. Once a situation of violence and oppression has been established, it engenders an entire way of life and behavior for those caught up in it—oppressors and oppressed alike. Both are submerged in this situation, and both bear the marks of oppression. Analysis of existential situations of oppression reveals that their inception lay in an act of violence—initiated by those with power. This violence, as a process, is perpetuated from generation to generation of oppressors, who become its heirs and are shaped in its climate. This climate creates in the oppressor a strongly possessive consciousness—possessive of the world and of men and women. Apart from direct, concrete, material possession of the world and of people, the oppressor consciousness could not understand itself—could not even exist. Fromm said of this consciousness that, without such possession, "it would lose contact with the world." The oppressor consciousness tends to transform everything surrounding it into an object of its domination. The earth, property, production, the creations of people, people themselves, time—everything is reduced to the status of objects at its disposal.

In their unrestrained eagerness to possess, the oppressors develop the conviction that it is possible for them to transform everything into objects of their purchasing power; hence their strictly materialistic concept of existence. Money is the measure of all things, and profit the primary goal. For the oppressors, what is worthwhile is to have more—always more—even at the cost of the oppressed having less or having nothing. For them, *to be is to have* and to be the class of the "haves."

As beneficiaries of a situation of oppression, the oppressors cannot perceive that if *having* is a condition of *being*, it is a necessary condition for all women and men. This is why their generosity is false. Humanity is a "thing," and they possess it as an exclusive right, as inherited property. To the oppressor consciousness, the humanization of the "others," of the people, appears not as the pursuit of full humanity, but as subversion.

The oppressors do not perceive their monopoly on *having more* as a privilege which dehumanizes others and themselves. They cannot see that, in the egoistic pursuit of *having* as a possessing class, they suffocate in their own possessions and no longer *are;* they merely *have.* For them, *having more* is an inalienable right, a right they acquired through their own "effort," with their "courage to take risks." If others do not have more, it is because they are incompetent and lazy, and worst of all is their unjustifiable ingratitude towards the "generous gestures" of the dominant class. Precisely because they are "ungrateful" and "envious," the oppressed are regarded as potential enemies who must be watched.

It could not be otherwise. If the humanization of the oppressed signifies subversion, so also does their freedom; hence the necessity for constant control. And the more the oppressors control the oppressed, the more they change them into apparently inanimate "things." This tendency of the oppressor consciousness to "in-animate" everything and everyone it encounters, in its eagerness to possess, unquestionably corresponds with a tendency to sadism.

> The pleasure in complete domination over another person (or other animate creature) is the very essence of the sadistic drive. Another way of formulating the same thought is to say that the aim of sadism is to transform a man into a thing, something animate into something inanimate, since by complete and absolute control the living loses one essential quality of life— freedom.[12]

Sadistic love is a perverted love—a love of death, not of life. One of the characteristics of the oppressor consciousness and its necrophilic view of the world is thus sadism. As the oppressor consciousness,

---

[12] Erich Fromm, *The Heart of Man* (New York, 1966), p. 32.

in order to dominate, tries to deter the drive to search, the restlessness, and the creative power which characterize life, it kills life. More and more, the oppressors are using science and technology as unquestionably powerful instruments for their purpose: the maintenance of the oppressive order through manipulation and repression.[13] The oppressed, as objects, as "things," have no purposes except those their oppressors prescribe for them.

Given the preceding context, another issue of indubitable importance arises: the fact that certain members of the oppressor class join the oppressed in their struggle for liberation, thus moving from one pole of the contradiction to the other. Theirs is a fundamental role, and has been so throughout the history of this struggle. It happens, however, that as they cease to be exploiters or indifferent spectators or simply the heirs of exploitation and move to the side of the exploited, they almost always bring with them the marks of their origin: their prejudices and their deformations, which include a lack of confidence in the people's ability to think, to want, and to know. Accordingly, these adherents to the people's cause constantly run the risk of falling into a type of generosity as malefic as that of the oppressors. The generosity of the oppressors is nourished by an unjust order, which must be maintained in order to justify that generosity. Our converts, on the other hand, truly desire to transform the unjust order; but because of their background they believe that they must be the executors of the transformation. They talk about the people, but they do not trust them; and trusting the people is the indispensable precondition for revolutionary change. A real humanist can be identified more by his trust in the people, which engages him in their struggle, than by a thousand actions in their favor without that trust.

Those who authentically commit themselves to the people must re-examine themselves constantly. This conversion is so radical as not to allow of ambiguous behavior. To affirm this commitment but to consider oneself the proprietor of revolutionary wisdom—which

---

[13] Regarding the "dominant forms of social control," see Herbert Marcuse, *One-Dimensional Man* (Boston, 1964) and *Eros and Civilization* (Boston, 1955).

must then be given to (or imposed on) the people—is to retain the old ways. The man or woman who proclaims devotion to the cause of liberation yet is unable to enter into *communion* with the people, whom he or she continues to regard as totally ignorant, is grievously self-deceived. The convert who approaches the people but feels alarm at each step they take, each doubt they express, and each suggestion they offer, and attempts to impose his "status," remains nostalgic towards his origins.

Conversion to the people requires a profound rebirth. Those who undergo it must take on a new form of existence; they can no longer remain as they were. Only through comradeship with the oppressed can the converts understand their characteristic ways of living and behaving, which in diverse moments reflect the structure of domination. One of these characteristics is the previously mentioned existential duality of the oppressed, who are at the same time themselves and the oppressor whose image they have internalized. Accordingly, until they concretely "discover" their oppressor and in turn their own consciousness, they nearly always express fatalistic attitudes towards their situation.

> The peasant begins to get courage to overcome his dependence when he realizes that he is dependent. Until then, he goes along with the boss and says "What can I do? I'm only a peasant."[14]

When superficially analyzed, this fatalism is sometimes interpreted as a docility that is a trait of national character. Fatalism in the guise of docility is the fruit of an historical and sociological situation, not an essential characteristic of a people's behavior. It almost always is related to the power of destiny or fate or fortune—inevitable forces—or to a distorted view of God. Under the sway of magic and myth, the oppressed (especially the peasants, who are almost submerged in nature)[15] see their suffering, the fruit of exploitation,

---

[14] Words of a peasant during an interview with the author.
[15] See Candido Mendes, *Memento dos vivos—A Esquerda católica no Brasil* (Rio, 1966).

as the  will of God—as if God were the creator of this "organized disorder."

Submerged in reality, the oppressed cannot perceive clearly the "order" which serves the interests of the oppressors whose image they have internalized. Chafing under the restrictions of this order, they often manifest a type of horizontal violence, striking out at their own comrades for the pettiest reasons.

> The colonized man will first manifest this aggressiveness which has been deposited in his bones against his own people. This is the period when the niggers beat each other up, and the police and magistrates do not know which way to turn when faced with the astonishing waves of crime in North Africa. . . . While the settler or the policeman has the right the livelong day to strike the native, to insult him and to make him crawl to them, you will see the native reaching for his knife at the slightest hostile or aggressive glance cast on him by another native; for the last resort of the native is to defend his personality vis-à-vis his brother.[16]

It is possible that in this behavior they are once more manifesting their duality. Because the oppressor exists within their oppressed comrades, when they attack those comrades they are indirectly attacking the oppressor as well.

On the other hand, at a certain point in their existential experience the oppressed feel an irresistible attraction towards the oppressors and their way of life. Sharing this way of life becomes an overpowering aspiration. In their alienation, the oppressed want at any cost to resemble the oppressors, to imitate them, to follow them. This phenomenon is especially prevalent in the middle-class oppressed, who yearn to be equal to the "eminent" men and women of the upper class. Albert Memmi, in an exceptional analysis of the "colonized mentality," refers to the contempt he felt towards the colonizer, mixed with "passionate" attraction towards him.

---

[16] Frantz Fanon, *The Wretched of the Earth* (New York, 1968), p. 52.

How could the colonizer look after his workers while periodically gunning down a crowd of colonized? How could the colonized deny himself so cruelly yet make such excessive demands? How could he hate the colonizers and yet admire them so passionately? (I too felt this admiration in spite of myself.)[17]

Self-depreciation is another characteristic of the oppressed, which derives from their internalization of the opinion the oppressors hold of them. So often do they hear that they are good for nothing, know nothing and are incapable of learning anything—that they are sick, lazy, and unproductive—that in the end they become convinced of their own unfitness.

The peasant feels inferior to the boss because the boss seems to be the only one who knows things and is able to run things.[18]

They call themselves ignorant and say the "professor" is the one who has knowledge and to whom they should listen. The criteria of knowledge imposed upon them are the conventional ones. "Why don't you," said a peasant participating in a culture circle,[19] "explain the pictures first? That way it'll take less time and won't give us a headache."

Almost never do they realize that they, too, "know things" they have learned in their relations with the world and with other women and men. Given the circumstances which have produced their duality, it is only natural that they distrust themselves.

Not infrequently, peasants in educational projects begin to discuss a generative theme in a lively manner, then stop suddenly and say to the educator: "Excuse us, we ought to keep quiet and let you talk. You are the one who knows, we don't know anything." They often insist that there is no difference between them and the animals; when they do admit a difference, it favors the animals. "They are freer than we are."

---

[17] *The Colonizer and the Colonized* (Boston, 1967), p. x.
[18] Words of a peasant during an interview with the author.
[19] See chapter 3, p. 113 ff.—Translator's note.

It is striking, however, to observe how this self-depreciation changes with the first changes in the situation of oppression. I heard a peasant leader say in an *asentamiento*[20] meeting, "They used to say we were unproductive because we were lazy and drunkards. All lies. Now that we are respected as men, we're going to show everyone that we were never drunkards or lazy. We were exploited!"

As long as their ambiguity persists, the oppressed are reluctant to resist, and totally lack confidence in themselves. They have a diffuse, magical belief in the invulnerability and power of the oppressor.[21] The magical force of the landowner's power holds particular sway in the rural areas. A sociologist friend of mine tells of a group of armed peasants in a Latin American country who recently took over a latifundium. For tactical reasons, they planned to hold the landowner as a hostage. But not one peasant had the courage to guard him; his very presence was terrifying. It is also possible that the act of opposing the boss provoked guilt feelings. In truth, the boss was "inside" them.

The oppressed must see examples of the vulnerability of the oppressor so that a contrary conviction can begin to grow within them. Until this occurs, they will continue disheartened, fearful, and beaten.[22] As long as the oppressed remain unaware of the causes of their condition, they fatalistically "accept" their exploitation. Further, they are apt to react in a passive and alienated manner when confronted with the necessity to struggle for their freedom and self-affirmation. Little by little, however, they tend to try out forms of rebellious action. In working towards liberation, one must neither lose sight of this passivity nor overlook the moment of awakening.

Within their unauthentic view of the world and of themselves, the oppressed feel like "things" owned by the oppressor. For the latter, *to be* is *to have,* almost always at the expense of those who have

---

[20] *Asentamiento* refers to a production unit of the Chilean agrarian reform experiment.—Translator's note.

[21] "The peasant has an almost instinctive fear of the boss." Interview with a peasant.

[22] See Regis Debray, *Revolution in the Revolution?* (New York, 1967).

nothing. For the oppressed, at a certain point in their existential experience, *to be* is not to resemble the oppressor, but *to be under* him, to depend on him. Accordingly, the oppressed are emotionally dependent.

> The peasant is a dependent. He can't say what he wants. Before he discovers his dependence, he suffers. He lets off steam at home, where he shouts at his children, beats them, and despairs. He complains about his wife and thinks everything is dreadful. He doesn't let off steam with the boss because he thinks the boss is a superior being. Lots of times, the peasant gives vent to his sorrows by drinking.[23]

This total emotional dependence can lead the oppressed to what Fromm calls necrophilic behavior: the destruction of life—their own or that of their oppressed fellows.

It is only when the oppressed find the oppressor out and become involved in the organized struggle for their liberation that they begin to believe in themselves. This discovery cannot be purely intellectual but must involve action; nor can it be limited to mere activism, but must include serious reflection: only then will it be a praxis.

Critical and liberating dialogue, which presupposes action, must be carried on with the oppressed at whatever the stage of their struggle for liberation.[24] The content of that dialogue can and should vary in accordance with historical conditions and the level at which the oppressed perceive reality. But to substitute monologue, slogans, and communiqués for dialogue is to attempt to liberate the oppressed with the instruments of domestication. Attempting to liberate the oppressed without their reflective participation in the act of liberation is to treat them as objects which must be saved from a burning building; it is to lead them into the populist pitfall and transform them into masses which can be manipulated.

At all stages of their liberation, the oppressed must see them-

---

[23] Interview with a peasant.

[24] Not in the open, of course; that would only provoke the fury of the oppressor and lead to still greater repression.

selves as women and men engaged in the ontological and historical vocation of becoming more fully human. Reflection and action become imperative when one does not erroneously attempt to dichotomize the content of humanity from its historical forms.

The insistence that the oppressed engage in reflection on their concrete situation is not a call to armchair revolution. On the contrary, reflection—true reflection—leads to action. On the other hand, when the situation calls for action, that action will constitute an authentic praxis only if its consequences become the object of critical reflection. In this sense, the praxis is the new *raison d'être* of the oppressed; and the revolution, which inaugurates the historical moment of this *raison d'être,* is not viable apart from their concomitant conscious involvement. Otherwise, action is pure activism.

To achieve this praxis, however, it is necessary to trust in the oppressed and in their ability to reason. Whoever lacks this trust will fail to initiate (or will abandon) dialogue, reflection, and communication, and will fall into using slogans, communiqués, monologues, and instructions. Superficial conversions to the cause of liberation carry this danger.

Political action on the side of the oppressed must be pedagogical action in the authentic sense of the word, and, therefore, action *with* the oppressed. Those who work for liberation must not take advantage of the emotional dependence of the oppressed— dependence that is the fruit of the concrete situation of domination which surrounds them and which engendered their unauthentic view of the world. Using their dependence to create still greater dependence is an oppressor tactic.

Libertarian action must recognize this dependence as a weak point and must attempt through reflection and action to transform it into independence. However, not even the best-intentioned leadership can bestow independence as a gift. The liberation of the oppressed is a liberation of women and men, not things. Accordingly, while no one liberates himself by his own efforts alone, neither is he liberated by others. Liberation, a human phenomenon, cannot be achieved by semihumans. Any attempt to treat people as semihumans only dehumanizes them. When people are already dehumanized, due to the oppression they suffer, the process of their liberation must not employ the methods of dehumanization.

The correct method for a revolutionary leadership to employ in the task of liberation is, therefore, *not* "libertarian propaganda." Nor can the leadership merely "implant" in the oppressed a belief in freedom, thus thinking to win their trust. The correct method lies in dialogue. The conviction of the oppressed that they must fight for their liberation is not a gift bestowed by the revolutionary leadership, but the result of their own *conscientização*.

The revolutionary leaders must realize that their own conviction of the necessity for struggle (an indispensable dimension of revolutionary wisdom) was not given to them by anyone else—if it is authentic. This conviction cannot be packaged and sold; it is reached, rather, by means of a totality of reflection and action. Only the leaders' own involvement in reality, within an historical situation, led them to criticize this situation and to wish to change it.

Likewise, the oppressed (who do not commit themselves to the struggle unless they are convinced, and who, if they do not make such a commitment, withhold the indispensable conditions for this struggle) must reach this conviction as Subjects, not as objects. They also must intervene critically in the situation which surrounds them and whose mark they bear; propaganda cannot achieve this. While the conviction of the necessity for struggle (without which the struggle is unfeasible) is indispensable to the revolutionary leadership (indeed, it was this conviction which constituted that leadership), it is also necessary for the oppressed. It is necessary, that is, unless one intends to carry out the transformation *for* the oppressed rather than *with* them. It is my belief that only the latter form of transformation is valid.[25]

The object in presenting these considerations is to defend the eminently pedagogical character of the revolution. The revolutionary leaders of every epoch who have affirmed that the oppressed must

---

[25] These points will be discussed at length in chapter 4.

accept the struggle for their liberation—an obvious point—have also thereby implicitly recognized the pedagogical aspect of this struggle. Many of these leaders, however (perhaps due to natural and understandable biases against pedagogy), have ended up using the "educational" methods employed by the oppressor. They deny pedagogical action in the liberation process, but they use propaganda to convince.

It is essential for the oppressed to realize that when they accept the struggle for humanization they also accept, from that moment, their total responsibility for the struggle. They must realize that they are fighting not merely for freedom from hunger, but for

> . . . freedom to create and to construct, to wonder and to venture. Such freedom requires that the individual be active and responsible, not a slave or a well-fed cog in the machine. . . . It is not enough that men are not slaves; if social conditions further the existence of automatons, the result will not be love of life, but love of death.[26]

The oppressed, who have been shaped by the death-affirming climate of oppression, must find through their struggle the way to life-affirming humanization, which does not lie *simply* in having more to eat (although it does involve having more to eat and cannot fail to include this aspect). The oppressed have been destroyed precisely because their situation has reduced them to things. In order to regain their humanity they must cease to be things and fight as men and women. This is a radical requirement. They cannot enter the struggle as objects in order *later* to become human beings.

The struggle begins with men's recognition that they have been destroyed. Propaganda, management, manipulation—all arms of domination—cannot be the instruments of their rehumanization. The only effective instrument is a humanizing pedagogy in which the revolutionary leadership establishes a permanent relationship of dialogue with the oppressed. In a humanizing pedagogy the method

---

[26] Fromm, *op. cit.*, pp. 52–53.

ceases to be an instrument by which the teachers (in this instance, the revolutionary leadership) can manipulate the students (in this instance, the oppressed), because it expresses the consciousness of the students themselves.

> The method is, in fact, the external form of consciousness manifest in acts, which takes on the fundamental property of consciousness—its intentionality. The essence of consciousness is being with the world, and this behavior is permanent and unavoidable. Accordingly, consciousness is in essence a 'way towards' something apart from itself, outside itself, which surrounds it and which it apprehends by means of its ideational capacity. Consciousness is thus by definition a method, in the most general sense of the word.[27]

A revolutionary leadership must accordingly practice *co-intentional* education. Teachers and students (leadership and people), co-intent on reality, are both Subjects, not only in the task of unveiling that reality, and thereby coming to know it critically, but in the task of re-creating that knowledge. As they attain this knowledge of reality through common reflection and action, they discover themselves as its permanent re-creators. In this way, the presence of the oppressed in the struggle for their liberation will be what it should be: not pseudo-participation, but committed involvement.

---

[27] Alvaro Vieira Pinto, from a work in preparation on the philosophy of science. I consider the quoted portion of great importance for the understanding of a problem-posing pedagogy (to be presented in chapter 2), and wish to thank Professor Vieira Pinto for permission to cite his work prior to publication.

# CHAPTER

# 2

A careful analysis of the teacher-student relationship at any level, inside or outside the school, reveals its fundamentally *narrative* character. This relationship involves a narrating Subject (the teacher) and patient, listening objects (the students). The contents, whether values or empirical dimensions of reality, tend in the process of being narrated to become lifeless and petrified. Education is suffering from narration sickness.

The teacher talks about reality as if it were motionless, static, compartmentalized, and predictable. Or else he expounds on a topic completely alien to the existential experience of the students. His task is to "fill" the students with the contents of his narration—contents which are detached from reality, disconnected from the totality that engendered them and could give them significance. Words are emptied of their concreteness and become a hollow, alienated, and alienating verbosity.

The outstanding characteristic of this narrative education, then, is the sonority of words, not their transforming power. "Four times four is sixteen; the capital of Pará is Belém." The student records, memorizes, and repeats these phrases without perceiving what four times four really means, or realizing the true significance of "capital" in the affirmation "the capital of Pará is Belém," that is, what Belém means for Pará and what Pará means for Brazil.

Narration (with the teacher as narrator) leads the students to memorize mechanically the narrated content. Worse yet, it turns them into "containers," into "receptacles" to be "filled" by the teacher. The more completely she fills the receptacles, the better a teacher she is. The more meekly the receptacles permit themselves to be filled, the better students they are.

Education thus becomes an act of depositing, in which the students are the depositories and the teacher is the depositor. Instead of communicating, the teacher issues communiqués and makes deposits which the students patiently receive, memorize, and repeat. This is the "banking" concept of education, in which the scope of action allowed to the students extends only as far as receiving, filing, and storing the deposits. They do, it is true, have the opportunity to become collectors or cataloguers of the things they store. But in the last analysis, it is the people themselves who are filed away through the lack of creativity, transformation, and knowledge in this (at best) misguided system. For apart from inquiry, apart from the praxis, individuals cannot be truly human. Knowledge emerges only through invention and re-invention, through the restless, impatient, continuing, hopeful inquiry human beings pursue in the world, with the world, and with each other.

In the banking concept of education, knowledge is a gift bestowed by those who consider themselves knowledgeable upon those whom they consider to know nothing. Projecting an absolute ignorance onto others, a characteristic of the ideology of oppression, negates education and knowledge as processes of inquiry. The teacher presents himself to his students as their necessary opposite; by considering their ignorance absolute, he justifies his own existence. The students, alienated like the slave in the Hegelian dialectic, accept their ignorance as justifying the teacher's existence—but, unlike the slave, they never discover that they educate the teacher.

The *raison d'être* of libertarian education, on the other hand, lies in its drive towards reconciliation. Education must begin with the solution of the teacher-student contradiction, by reconciling the poles of the contradiction so that both are simultaneously teachers *and* students.

This solution is not (nor can it be) found in the banking concept. On the contrary, banking education maintains and even stimulates the contradiction through the following attitudes and practices, which mirror oppressive society as a whole:

(a)　the teacher teaches and the students are taught;
(b)　the teacher knows everything and the students know nothing;
(c)　the teacher thinks and the students are thought about;
(d)　the teacher talks and the students listen—meekly;
(e)　the teacher disciplines and the students are disciplined;
(f)　the teacher chooses and enforces his choice, and the students comply;
(g)　the teacher acts and the students have the illusion of acting through the action of the teacher;
(h)　the teacher chooses the program content, and the students (who were not consulted) adapt to it;
(i)　the teacher confuses the authority of knowledge with his or her own professional authority, which she and he sets in opposition to the freedom of the students;
(j)　the teacher is the Subject of the learning process, while the pupils are mere objects.

It is not surprising that the banking concept of education regards men as adaptable, manageable beings. The more students work at storing the deposits entrusted to them, the less they develop the critical consciousness which would result from their intervention in the world as transformers of that world. The more completely they accept the passive role imposed on them, the more they tend simply to adapt to the world as it is and to the fragmented view of reality deposited in them.

The capability of banking education to minimize or annul the students' creative power and to stimulate their credulity serves the interests of the oppressors, who care neither to have the world revealed nor to see it transformed. The oppressors use their "humanitarianism" to preserve a profitable situation. Thus they react almost instinctively against any experiment in education which stimulates the critical faculties and is not content with a partial view of reality but always seeks out the ties which link one point to another and one problem to another.

Indeed, the interests of the oppressors lie in "changing the consciousness of the oppressed, not the situation which oppresses them";[1] for the more the oppressed can be led to adapt to that situation, the more easily they can be dominated. To achieve this end, the oppressors use the banking concept of education in conjunction with a paternalistic social action apparatus, within which the oppressed receive the euphemistic title of "welfare recipients." They are treated as individual cases, as marginal persons who deviate from the general configuration of a "good, organized, and just" society. The oppressed are regarded as the pathology of the healthy society, which must therefore adjust these "incompetent and lazy" folk to its own patterns by changing their mentality. These marginals need to be "integrated," "incorporated" into the healthy society that they have "forsaken."

The truth is, however, that the oppressed are not "marginals," are not people living "outside" society. They have always been "inside"—inside the structure which made them "beings for others." The solution is not to "integrate" them into the structure of oppression, but to transform that structure so that they can become "beings for themselves." Such transformation, of course, would undermine the oppressors' purposes; hence their utilization of the banking concept of education to avoid the threat of student *conscientização*.

The banking approach to adult education, for example, will never propose to students that they critically consider reality. It will deal instead with such vital questions as whether Roger gave green grass to the goat, and insist upon the importance of learning that, on the contrary, Roger gave green grass to the rabbit. The "humanism" of the banking approach masks the effort to turn women and men into automatons—the very negation of their ontological vocation to be more fully human.

---

[1] Simone de Beauvoir, *La Pensée de Droite, Aujord'hui* (Paris); ST, *El Pensamiento político de la Derecha* (Buenos Aires, 1963), p. 34.

Those who use the banking approach, knowingly or unknowingly (for there are innumerable well-intentioned bank-clerk teachers who do not realize that they are serving only to dehumanize), fail to perceive that the deposits themselves contain contradictions about reality. But, sooner or later, these contradictions may lead formerly passive students to turn against their domestication and the attempt to domesticate reality. They may discover through existential experience that their present way of life is irreconcilable with their vocation to become fully human. They may perceive through their relations with reality that reality is really a *process*, undergoing constant transformation. If men and women are searchers and their ontological vocation is humanization, sooner or later they may perceive the contradiction in which banking education seeks to maintain them, and then engage themselves in the struggle for their liberation.

But the humanist, revolutionary educator cannot wait for this possibility to materialize. From the outset, her efforts must coincide with those of the students to engage in critical thinking and the quest for mutual humanization. His efforts must be imbued with a profound trust in people and their creative power. To achieve this, they must be partners of the students in their relations with them.

The banking concept does not admit to such partnership—and necessarily so. To resolve the teacher-student contradiction, to exchange the role of depositor, prescriber, domesticator, for the role of student among students would be to undermine the power of oppression and serve the cause of liberation.

Implicit in the banking concept is the assumption of a dichotomy between human beings and the world: a person is merely *in* the world, not *with* the world or with others; the individual is spectator, not re-creator. In this view, the person is not a conscious being (*corpo consciente*); he or she is rather the possessor of *a* consciousness: an empty "mind" passively open to the reception of deposits of reality from the world outside. For example, my desk, my books, my coffee cup, all the objects before me—as bits of the world which surround me—would be "inside" me, exactly as I am inside my study right now. This view makes no distinction between being accessible to consciousness and entering consciousness. The distinction, however, is essential: the objects which surround me are simply accessible to my consciousness, not located within it. I am aware of them, but they are not inside me.

It follows logically from the banking notion of consciousness that the educator's role is to regulate the way the world "enters into" the students. The teacher's task is to organize a process which already occurs spontaneously, to "fill" the students by making deposits of information which he or she considers to constitute true knowledge.[2] And since people "receive" the world as passive entities, education should make them more passive still, and adapt them to the world. The educated individual is the adapted person, because she or he is better "fit" for the world. Translated into practice, this concept is well suited to the purposes of the oppressors, whose tranquility rests on how well people fit the world the oppressors have created, and how little they question it.

The more completely the majority adapt to the purposes which the dominant minority prescribe for them (thereby depriving them of the right to their own purposes), the more easily the minority can continue to prescribe. The theory and practice of banking education serve this end quite efficiently. Verbalistic lessons, reading requirements,[3] the methods for evaluating "knowledge," the distance between the teacher and the taught, the criteria for promotion: everything in this ready-to-wear approach serves to obviate thinking.

The bank-clerk educator does not realize that there is no true security in his hypertrophied role, that one must seek to live *with* others in solidarity. One cannot impose oneself, nor even merely

---

[2] This concept corresponds to what Sartre calls the "digestive" or "nutritive" concept of education, in which knowledge is "fed" by the teacher to the students to "fill them out." See Jean-Paul Sartre, "Une idée fundamentale de la phénoménologie de Husserl: L'intentionalité," *Situations I* (Paris. 1947).

[3] For example, some professors specify in their reading lists that a book should be read from pages 10 to 15—and do this to "help" their students!

co-exist with one's students. Solidarity requires true communication, and the concept by which such an educator is guided fears and proscribes communication.

Yet only through communication can human life hold meaning. The teacher's thinking is authenticated only by the authenticity of the students' thinking. The teacher cannot think for her students, nor can she impose her thought on them. Authentic thinking, thinking that is concerned about *reality,* does not take place in ivory tower isolation, but only in communication. If it is true that thought has meaning only when generated by action upon the world, the subordination of students to teachers becomes impossible.

Because banking education begins with a false understanding of men and women as objects, it cannot promote the development of what Fromm calls "biophily," but instead produces its opposite: "necrophily."

> While life is characterized by growth in a structured, functional manner, the necrophilous person loves all that does not grow, all that is mechanical. The necrophilous person is driven by the desire to transform the organic into the inorganic, to approach life mechanically, as if all living persons were things. . . . Memory, rather than experience; having, rather than being, is what counts. The necrophilous person can relate to an object—a flower or a person—only if he possesses it; hence a threat to his possession is a threat to himself; if he loses possession he loses contact with the world. . . . He loves control, and in the act of controlling he kills life.[4]

Oppression—overwhelming control—is necrophilic; it is nourished by love of death, not life. The banking concept of education, which serves the interests of oppression, is also necrophilic. Based on a mechanistic, static, naturalistic, spatialized view of consciousness, it transforms students into receiving objects. It attempts to control thinking and action, leads women and men to adjust to the world, and inhibits their creative power.

---

[4] Fromm, *op. cit.,* p. 41.

When their efforts to act responsibly are frustrated, when they find themselves unable to use their faculties, people suffer. "This suffering due to impotence is rooted in the very fact that the human equilibrium has been disturbed."[5] But the inability to act which causes people's anguish also causes them to reject their impotence, by attempting

> . . . to restore [their] capacity to act. But can [they], and how? One way is to submit to and identify with a person or group having power. By this symbolic participation in another person's life, [men have] the illusion of acting, when in reality [they] only submit to and become a part of those who act.[6]

Populist manifestations perhaps best exemplify this type of behavior by the oppressed, who, by identifying with charismatic leaders, come to feel that they themselves are active and effective. The rebellion they express as they emerge in the historical process is motivated by that desire to act effectively. The dominant elites consider the remedy to be more domination and repression, carried out in the name of freedom, order, and social peace (that is, the peace of the elites). Thus they can condemn—logically, from their point of view—"the violence of a strike by workers and [can] call upon the state in the same breath to use violence in putting down the strike."[7]

Education as the exercise of domination stimulates the credulity of students, with the ideological intent (often not perceived by educators) of indoctrinating them to adapt to the world of oppression. This accusation is not made in the naïve hope that the dominant elites will thereby simply abandon the practice. Its objective is to call the attention of true humanists to the fact that they cannot use banking educational methods in the pursuit of liberation, for they would only negate that very pursuit. Nor may a revolutionary society inherit these methods from an oppressor society. The revolutionary society which practices banking education is either misguided or

---

[5] *Ibid.*, p. 31.
[6] *Ibid.*
[7] Reinhold Niebuhr, *Moral Man and Immoral Society* (New York, 1960), p. 130.

mistrusting of people. In either event, it is threatened by the specter of reaction.

Unfortunately, those who espouse the cause of liberation are themselves surrounded and influenced by the climate which generates the banking concept, and often do not perceive its true significance or its dehumanizing power. Paradoxically, then, they utilize this same instrument of alienation in what they consider an effort to liberate. Indeed, some "revolutionaries" brand as "innocents," "dreamers," or even "reactionaries" those who would challenge this educational practice. But one does not liberate people by alienating them. Authentic liberation—the process of humanization—is not another deposit to be made in men. Liberation is a praxis: the action and reflection of men and women upon their world in order to transform it. Those truly committed to the cause of liberation can accept neither the mechanistic concept of consciousness as an empty vessel to be filled, nor the use of banking methods of domination (propaganda, slogans—deposits) in the name of liberation.

Those truly committed to liberation must reject the banking concept in its entirety, adopting instead a concept of women and men as conscious beings, and consciousness as consciousness intent upon the world. They must abandon the educational goal of deposit-making and replace it with the posing of the problems of human beings in their relations with the world. "Problem-posing" education, responding to the essence of consciousness—*intentionality*—rejects communiqués and embodies communication. It epitomizes the special characteristic of consciousness: being *conscious of,* not only as intent on objects but as turned in upon itself in a Jasperian "split"—consciousness as consciousness *of* consciousness.

Liberating education consists in acts of cognition, not transferrals of information. It is a learning situation in which the cognizable object (far from being the end of the cognitive act) intermediates the cognitive actors—teacher on the one hand and students on the other. Accordingly, the practice of problem-posing education entails at the outset that the teacher-student contradiction to be resolved. Dialogical relations—indispensable to the capacity of cognitive actors to cooperate in perceiving the same cognizable object—are otherwise impossible.

Indeed, problem-posing education, which breaks with the vertical patterns characteristic of banking education, can fulfill its function as the practice of freedom only if it can overcome the above contradiction. Through dialogue, the teacher-of-the-students and the students-of-the-teacher cease to exist and a new term emerges: teacher-student with students-teachers. The teacher is no longer merely the-one-who-teaches, but one who is himself taught in dialogue with the students, who in turn while being taught also teach. They become jointly responsible for a process in which all grow. In this process, arguments based on "authority" are no longer valid; in order to function, authority must be *on the side of* freedom, not *against* it. Here, no one teaches another, nor is anyone self-taught. People teach each other, mediated by the world, by the cognizable objects which in banking education are "owned" by the teacher.

The banking concept (with its tendency to dichotomize everything) distinguishes two stages in the action of the educator. During the first, he cognizes a cognizable object while he prepares his lessons in his study or his laboratory; during the second, he expounds to his students about that object. The students are not called upon to know, but to memorize the contents narrated by the teacher. Nor do the students practice any act of cognition, since the object towards which that act should be directed is the property of the teacher rather than a medium evoking the critical reflection of both teacher and students. Hence in the name of the "preservation of culture and knowledge" we have a system which achieves neither true knowledge nor true culture.

The problem-posing method does not dichotomize the activity of the teacher-student: she is not "cognitive" at one point and "narrative" at another. She is always "cognitive," whether preparing a project or engaging in dialogue with the students. He does not regard cognizable objects as his private property, but as the object of reflection by himself and the students. In this way, the problem-posing educator constantly re-forms his reflections in the reflection of the students. The students—no longer docile listeners—are now critical co-investigators in dialogue with the teacher. The teacher presents the material to the students for their consideration, and re-considers her earlier considerations as the students express their own. The role of the problem-posing educator is to create; together with the students, the conditions under which knowledge at the level of the *doxa* is superseded by true knowledge, at the level of the *logos*.

Whereas banking education anesthetizes and inhibits creative power, problem-posing education involves a constant unveiling of reality. The former attempts to maintain the *submersion* of consciousness; the latter strives for the *emergence* of consciousness and *critical intervention* in reality.

Students, as they are increasingly posed with problems relating to themselves in the world and with the world, will feel increasingly challenged and obliged to respond to that challenge. Because they apprehend the challenge as interrelated to other problems within a total context, not as a theoretical question, the resulting comprehension tends to be increasingly critical and thus constantly less alienated. Their response to the challenge evokes new challenges, followed by new understandings; and gradually the students come to regard themselves as committed.

Education as the practice of freedom—as opposed to education as the practice of domination—denies that man is abstract, isolated, independent, and unattached to the world; it also denies that the world exists as a reality apart from people. Authentic reflection considers neither abstract man nor the world without people, but people in their relations with the world. In these relations consciousness and world are simultaneous: consciousness neither precedes the world nor follows it.

> La conscience et le monde sont donnés d'un même coup: extérieur par essence à la conscience, le monde est, par essence relatif à elle.[8]

---

[8] Sartre; *op. cit.*, p. 32.

In one of our culture circles in Chile, the group was discussing (based on a codification[9]) the anthropological concept of culture. In the midst of the discussion, a peasant who by banking standards was completely ignorant said: "Now I see that without man there is no world." When the educator responded: "Let's say, for the sake of argument, that all the men on earth were to die, but that the earth itself remained, together with trees, birds, animals, rivers, seas, the stars . . . wouldn't all this be a world?" "Oh no," the peasant replied emphatically. "There would be no one to say: 'This is a world.'"

The peasant wished to express the idea that there would be lacking the consciousness of the world which necessarily implies the world of consciousness. *I* cannot exist without a *non-I*. In turn, the *not-I* depends on that existence. The world which brings consciousness into existence becomes the world *of* that consciousness. Hence, the previously cited affirmation of Sartre: "*La conscience et le monde sont donnés d'un même coup.*"

As women and men, simultaneously reflecting on themselves and on the world, increase the scope of their perception, they begin to direct their observations towards previously inconspicuous phenomena:

> In perception properly so-called, as an explicit awareness [*Gewahren*], I am turned towards the object, to the paper, for instance. I apprehend it as being this here and now. The apprehension is a singling out, every object having a background in experience. Around and about the paper lie books, pencils, inkwell, and so forth, and these in a certain sense are also "perceived", perceptually there, in the "field of intuition"; but whilst I was turned towards the paper there was no turning in their direction, nor any apprehending of them, not even in a secondary sense. They appeared and yet were not singled out, were not posited on their own account. Every perception of a thing has such a zone of background intuitions or background awareness, if "intuiting" already includes the state of being turned towards, and this also is a "conscious experience", or more briefly

---

[9]  See chapter 3.—Translator's note.

a "consciousness of" all indeed that in point of fact lies in the co-perceived objective background.[10]

That which had existed objectively but had not been perceived in its deeper implications (if indeed it was perceived at all) begins to "stand out," assuming the character of a problem and therefore of challenge. Thus, men and women begin to single out elements from their "background awareness" and to reflect upon them. These elements are now objects of their consideration, and, as such, objects oftheir action and cognition.

In problem-posing education, people develop their power to perceive critically *the way they exist* in the world *with which* and *in which* they find themselves; they come to see the world not as a static reality, but as a reality in process, in transformation. Although the dialectical relations of women and men with the world exist independently of how these relations are perceived (or whether or not they are perceived at all), it is also true that the form of action they adopt is to a large extent a function of how they perceive themselves in the world. Hence, the teacher-student and the students-teachers reflect simultaneously on themselves and the world without dichotomizing this reflection from action, and thus establish an authentic form of thought and action.

Once again, the two educational concepts and practices under analysis come into conflict. Banking education (for obvious reasons) attempts, by mythicizing reality, to conceal certain facts which explain the way human beings exist in the world; problem-posing education sets itself the task of demythologizing. Banking education resists dialogue; problem-posing education regards dialogue as indispensable to the act of cognition which unveils reality. Banking education treats students as objects of assistance; problem-posing education makes them critical thinkers. Banking education inhibits creativity and domesticates (although it cannot completely destroy) the *intentionality* of consciousness by isolating consciousness from

---

[10] Edmund Husserl, *Ideas—General Introduction to Pure Phenomenology* (London, 1969), pp. 105–106.

the world, thereby denying people their ontological and historical vocation of becoming more fully human. Problem-posing education bases itself on creativity and stimulates true reflection and action upon reality, thereby responding to the vocation of persons as beings who are authentic only when engaged in inquiry and creative transformation. In sum: banking theory and practice, as immobilizing and fixating forces, fail to acknowledge men and women as historical beings; problem-posing theory and practice take the people's historicity as their starting point.

Problem-posing education affirms men and women as beings in the process of *becoming*—as unfinished, uncompleted beings in and with a likewise unfinished reality. Indeed, in contrast to other animals who are unfinished, but not historical, people know themselves to be unfinished; they are aware of their incompletion. In this incompletion and this awareness lie the very roots of education as an exclusively human manifestation. The unfinished character of human beings and the transformational character of reality necessitate that education be an ongoing activity.

Education is thus constantly remade in the praxis. In order to *be,* it must *become.* Its "duration" (in the Bergsonian meaning of the word) is found in the interplay of the opposites *permanence* and *change.* The banking method emphasizes permanence and becomes reactionary; problem-posing education—which accepts neither a "well-behaved" present nor a predetermined future—roots itself in the dynamic present and becomes revolutionary.

Problem-posing education is revolutionary futurity. Hence it is prophetic (and, as such, hopeful). Hence, it corresponds to the historical nature of humankind. Hence, it affirms women and men as beings who transcend themselves, who move forward and look ahead, for whom immobility represents a fatal threat, for whom looking at the past must only be a means of understanding more clearly what and who they are so that they can more wisely build the future. Hence, it identifies with the movement which engages people as beings aware of their incompletion—an historical movement which has its point of departure, its Subjects and its objective.

The point of departure of the movement lies in the people them-selves. But since people do not exist apart from the world, apart from reality, the movement must begin with the human-world rela-tionship. Accordingly, the point of departure must always be with men and women in the "here and now," which constitutes the situ-ation within which they are submerged, from which they emerge, and in which they intervene. Only by starting from this situation—which determines their perception of it—can they begin to move. To do this authentically they must perceive their state not as fated and unalterable, but merely as limiting—and therefore challenging.

Whereas the banking method directly or indirectly reinforces men's fatalistic perception of their situation, the problem-posing method presents this very situation to them as a problem. As the situation becomes the object of their cognition, the naïve or magical perception which produced their fatalism gives way to perception which is able to perceive itself even as it perceives reality, and can thus be critically objective about that reality.

A deepened consciousness of their situation leads people to ap-prehend that situation as an historical reality susceptible of transfor-mation. Resignation gives way to the drive for transformation and inquiry, over which men feel themselves to be in control. If people, as historical beings necessarily engaged with other people in a move-ment of inquiry, did not control that movement, it would be (and is) a violation of their humanity. Any situation in which some indi-viduals prevent others from engaging in the process of inquiry is one of violence. The means used are not important; to alienate human beings from their own decision-making is to change them into objects.

This movement of inquiry must be directed towards humaniza-tion—the people's historical vocation. The pursuit of full humanity, however, cannot be carried out in isolation or individualism, but only in fellowship and solidarity; therefore it cannot unfold in the antagonistic relations between oppressors and oppressed. No one can be authentically human while he prevents others from being so. Attempting *to be more* human, individualistically, leads to *having more,* egotistically, a form of dehumanization. Not that it is not fundamental *to have* in order *to be* human. Precisely because it is necessary, some men's *having* must not be allowed to constitute an obstacle to others' *having,* must not consolidate the power of the former to crush the latter.

Problem-posing education, as a humanist and liberating praxis, posits as fundamental that the people subjected to domination must fight for their emancipation. To that end, it enables teachers and students to become Subjects of the educational process by overcoming authoritarianism and an alienating intellectualism; it also enables people to overcome their false perception of reality. The world—no longer something to be described with deceptive words—becomes the object of that transforming action by men and women which results in their humanization.

Problem-posing education does not and cannot serve the interests of the oppressor. No oppressive order could permit the oppressed to begin to question: Why? While only a revolutionary society can carry out this education in systematic terms, the revolutionary leaders need not take full power before they can employ the method. In the revolutionary process, the leaders cannot utilize the banking method as an interim measure, justified on grounds of expediency, with the intention of *later* behaving in a genuinely revolutionary fashion. They must be revolutionary—that is to say, dialogical—from the outset.

# CHAPTER

# 3

As we attempt to analyze dialogue as a human phenomenon, we discover something which is the essence of dialogue itself: *the word*. But the word is more than just an instrument which makes dialogue possible; accordingly, we must seek its constitutive elements. Within the word we find two dimensions, reflection and action, in such radical interaction that if one is sacrificed—even in part—the other immediately suffers. There is no true word that is not at the same time a praxis.[1] Thus, to speak a true word is to transform the world.[2]

An unauthentic word, one which is unable to transform reality, results when dichotomy is imposed upon its constitutive elements. When a word is deprived of its dimension of action, reflection automatically suffers as well; and the word is changed into idle chatter, into *verbalism*, into an alienated and alienating "blah." It becomes an empty word, one which cannot denounce the world, for denunciation is impossible without a commitment to transform, and there is no transformation without action.

---

[1] Action  
Reflection $\Big\}$ word = work = praxis  
Sacrifice of action = verbalism  
Sacrifice of reflection = activism

[2] Some of these reflections emerged as a result of conversations with Professor Ernani Maria Fiori.

On the other hand, if action is emphasized exclusively, to the detriment of reflection, the word is converted into *activism*. The latter—action for action's sake—negates the true praxis and makes dialogue impossible. Either dichotomy, by creating unauthentic forms of existence, creates also unauthentic forms of thought, which reinforce the original dichotomy.

Human existence cannot be silent, nor can it be nourished by false words, but only by true words, with which men and women transform the world. To exist, humanly, is to *name* the world, to change it. Once named, the world in its turn reappears to the namers as a problem and requires of them a new *naming*. Human beings are not built in silence,[3] but in word, in work, in action-reflection.

But while to say the true word—which is work, which is praxis—is to transform the world, saying that word is not the privilege of some few persons, but the right of everyone. Consequently, no one can say a true word alone—nor can she say it *for* another, in a prescriptive act which robs others of their words.

Dialogue is the encounter between men, mediated by the world, in order to name the world. Hence, dialogue cannot occur between those who want to name the world and those who do not wish this naming—between those who deny others the right to speak their word and those whose right to speak has been denied them. Those who have been denied their primordial right to speak their word must first reclaim this right and prevent the continuation of this dehumanizing aggression.

If it is in speaking their word that people, by naming the world, transform it, dialogue imposes itself as the way by which they achieve significance as human beings. Dialogue is thus an existential necessity. And since dialogue is the encounter in which the united reflection and action of the dialoguers are addressed to the world which

---

[3] I obviously do not refer to the silence of profound meditation, in which men only apparently leave the world, withdrawing from it in order to consider it in its totality, and thus remaining with it. But this type of retreat is only authentic when the meditator is "bathed" in reality; not when the retreat signifies contempt for the world and flight from it, in a type of "historical schizophrenia."

is to be transformed and humanized, this dialogue cannot be reduced to the act of one person's "depositing" ideas in another, nor canit become a simple exchange of ideas to be "consumed" by the discussants. Nor yet is it a hostile, polemical argument between those who are committed neither to the naming of the world, nor to the search for truth, but rather to the imposition of their own truth. Because dialogue is an encounter among women and men who name the world, it must not be a situation where some name on behalf of others. It is an act of creation; it must not serve as a crafty instrument for the domination of one person by another. The domination implicit in dialogue is that of the world by the dialoguers; it is conquest of the world for the liberation of humankind.

Dialogue cannot exist, however, in the absence of a profound love for the world and for people. The naming of the world, which is an act of creation and re-creation, is not possible if it is not infused with love.[4] Love is at the same time the foundation of dialogue and dialogue itself. It is thus necessarily the task of responsible Subjects and cannot exist in a relation of domination. Domination reveals the pathology of love: sadism in the dominator and masochism in the dominated. Because love is an act of courage, not of fear, love is commitment to others. No matter where the oppressed are found, the act of love is commitment to their cause—the cause of liberation. And this commitment, because it is loving, is dialogical. As an act

---

[4] I am more and more convinced that true revolutionaries must perceive the revolution, because of its creative and liberating nature, as an act of love. For me, the revolution, which is not possible without a theory of revolution—and therefore science—is not irreconcilable with love. On the contrary: the revolution is made by people to achieve their humanization. What, indeed, is the deeper motive which moves individuals to become revolutionaries, but the dehumanization of people? The distortion imposed on the word "love" by the capitalist world cannot prevent the revolution from being essentially loving in character, nor can it prevent the revolutionaries from affirming their love of life. Guevara (while admitting the "risk of seeming ridiculous") was not afraid to affirm it: "Let me say, with the risk of appearing ridiculous, that the true revolutionary is guided by strong feelings of love. It is impossible to think of an authentic revolutionary without this quality." *Venceremos—The Speeches and Writings of Che Guevara,* edited by John Gerassi (New York, 1969), p. 398.

of bravery, love cannot be sentimental; as an act of freedom, it must not serve as a pretext for manipulation. It must generate other acts of freedom; otherwise, it is not love. Only by abolishing the situation of oppression is it possible to restore the love which that situation made impossible. If I do not love the world—if I do not love life—if I do not love people—I cannot enter into dialogue.

On the other hand, dialogue cannot exist without humility. The naming of the world, through which people constantly re-create that world, cannot be an act of arrogance. Dialogue, as the encounter of those addressed to the common task of learning and acting, is broken if the parties (or one of them) lack humility. How can I dialogue if I always project ignorance onto others and never perceive my own? How can I dialogue if I regard myself as a case apart from others—mere "its" in whom I cannot recognize other "I"s? How can I dialogue if I consider myself a member of the in-group of "pure" men, the owners of truth and knowledge, for whom all non-members are "these people" or "the great unwashed"? How can I dialogue if I start from the premise that naming the world is the task of an elite and that the presence of the people in history is a sign of deterioration, thus to be avoided? How can I dialogue if I am closed to—and even offended by—the contribution of others? How can I dialogue if I am afraid of being displaced, the mere possibility causing me torment and weakness? Self-sufficiency is incompatible with dialogue. Men and women who lack humility (or have lost it) cannot come to the people, cannot be their partners in naming the world. Someone who cannot acknowledge himself to be as mortal as everyone else still has a long way to go before he can reach the point of encounter. At the point of encounter there are neither utter ignoramuses nor perfect sages; there are only people who are attempting, together, to learn more than they now know.

Dialogue further requires an intense faith in humankind, faith in their power to make and remake, to create and re-create, faith in their vocation to be more fully human (which is not the privilege of an elite, but the birthright of all). Faith in people is an *a priori* requirement for dialogue; the "dialogical man" believes in others even before he meets them face to face. His faith, however, is not naïve. The "dialogical man" is critical and knows that although it is within the power of humans to create and transform, in a concrete situation of alienation individuals may be impaired in the use of that power. Far from destroying his faith in the people, however, this possibility strikes him as a challenge to which he must respond. He is convinced that the power to create and transform, even when thwarted in concrete situations, tends to be reborn. And that rebirth can occur—not gratuitously, but in and through the struggle for liberation—in the supersedence of slave labor by emancipated labor which gives zest to life. Without this faith in people, dialogue is a farce which inevitably degenerates into paternalistic manipulation.

Founding itself upon love, humility, and faith, dialogue becomes a horizontal relationship of which mutual trust between the dialoguers is the logical consequence. It would be a contradiction in terms if dialogue—loving, humble, and full of faith—did not produce this climate of mutual trust, which leads the dialoguers into ever closer partnership in the naming of the world. Conversely, such trust is obviously absent in the anti-dialogics of the banking method of education. Whereas faith in humankind is an *a priori* requirement for dialogue, trust is established by dialogue. Should it founder, it will be seen that the preconditions were lacking. False love, false humility, and feeble faith in others cannot create trust. Trust is contingent on the evidence which one party provides the others of his true, concrete intentions; it cannot exist if that party's words do not coincide with their actions. To say one thing and do another—to take one's own word lightly—cannot inspire trust. To glorify democracy and to silence the people is a farce; to discourse on humanism and to negate people is a lie.

Nor yet can dialogue exist without hope. Hope is rooted in men's incompletion, from which they move out in constant search—a search which can be carried out only in communion with others. Hopelessness is a form of silence, of denying the world and fleeing from it. The dehumanization resulting from an unjust order is not a cause for despair but for hope, leading to the incessant pursuit of the humanity denied by injustice. Hope, however, does not consist in crossing one's arms and waiting. As long as I fight, I am moved by hope; and if I fight with hope, then I can wait. As the encounter of women and men seeking to be more fully human, dialogue cannot be carried on in a climate of hopelessness. If the dialoguers expect nothing to come of their efforts, their encounter will be empty and sterile, bureaucratic and tedious.

Finally, true dialogue cannot exist unless the dialoguers engage in critical thinking—thinking which discerns an indivisible solidarity between the world and the people and admits of no dichotomy between them—thinking which perceives reality as process, as transformation, rather than as a static entity—thinking which does not separate itself from action, but constantly immerses itself in temporality without fear of the risks involved. Critical thinking contrasts with naive thinking, which sees "historical time as a weight, a stratification of the acquisitions and experiences of the past,"[5] from which the present should emerge normalized and "well-behaved." For the naive thinker, the important thing is accommodation to this normalized "today." For the critic, the important thing is the continuing transformation of reality, in behalf of the continuing humanization of men. In the words of Pierre Furter:

> The goal will no longer be to eliminate the risks of temporality by clutching to guaranteed space, but rather to temporalize space . . . The universe is revealed to me not as space, imposing a massive presence to which I can but adapt, but as a scope, a domain which takes shape as I act upon it.[6]

For naïve thinking, the goal is precisely to hold fast to this guaranteed space and adjust to it. By thus denying temporality, it denies itself as well.

Only dialogue, which requires critical thinking, is also capable of generating critical thinking. Without dialogue there is no communi-

---

[5]  From the letter of a friend.
[6]  Pierre Furter, *Educação e Vida* (Rio, 1966), pp. 26–27.

cation, and without communication there can be no true education. Education which is able to resolve the contradiction between teacher and student takes place in a situation in which both address their act of cognition to the object by which they are mediated. Thus, the dialogical character of education as the practice of freedom does not begin when the teacher-student meets with the students-teachers in a pedagogical situation, but rather when the former first asks herself or himself *what* she or he will dialogue with the latter *about*. And preoccupation with the content of dialogue is really preoccupation with the program content of education.

For the anti-dialogical banking educator, the question of content simply concerns the program about which he will discourse to his students; and he answers his own question, by organizing his own program. For the dialogical, problem-posing teacher-student, the program content of education is neither a gift nor an imposition—bits of information to be deposited in the students—but rather the organized, systematized, and developed "re-presentation" to individuals of the things about which they want to know more.[7]

Authentic education is not carried on by "A" *for* "B" or by "A" *about* "B," but rather by "A" *with* "B," mediated by the world—a world which impresses and challenges both parties, giving rise to views or opinions about it. These views, impregnated with anxieties, doubts, hopes, or hopelessness, imply significant themes on the basis of which the program content of education can be built. In its desire to create an ideal model of the "good man," a naïvely conceived humanism often overlooks the concrete, existential, present situation of real people. Authentic humanism, in Pierre Furter's words, "consists in permitting the emergence of the awareness of our full humanity, as a condition and as an obligation, as a situation

---

[7] In a long conversation with Malraux, Mao-Tse-Tung declared, "You know I've proclaimed for a long time: we must teach the masses clearly what we have received from them confusedly." André Malraux, *Anti-Memoirs* (New York, 1968), pp. 361–362. This affirmation contains an entire dialogical theory of how to construct the program content of education, which cannot be elaborated according to what the *educator* thinks best for the *students*.

and as a project."[8] We simply cannot go to the laborers—urban or peasant[9]—in the banking style, to give them "knowledge" or to impose upon them the model of the "good man" contained in a program whose content we have ourselves organized. Many political and educational plans have failed because their authors designed them according to their own personal views of reality, never once taking into account (except as mere objects of their actions) the *men-in-a-situation* to whom their program was ostensibly directed.

For the truly humanist educator and the authentic revolutionary, the object of action is the reality to be transformed by them together with other people—not other men and women themselves. The oppressors are the ones who act upon the people to indoctrinate them and adjust them to a reality which must remain untouched. Unfortunately, however, in their desire to obtain the support of the people for revolutionary action, revolutionary leaders often fall for the banking line of planning program content from the top down. They approach the peasant or urban masses with projects which may correspond to their own view of the world, but not to that of the people.[10] They forget that their fundamental objective is to fight

---

[8]  Furter, *op. cit.*, p. 165.

[9]  The latter, usually submerged in a colonial context, are almost umbilically linked to the world of nature, in relation to which they feel themselves to be component parts rather than shapers.

[10]  "Our cultural workers must serve the people with great enthusiasm and devotion, and they must link themselves with the masses, not divorce themselves from the masses. In order to do so, they must act in accordance with the needs and wishes of the masses. All work done for the masses must start from their needs and not from the desire of any individual, however well-intentioned. It often happens that objectively the masses need a certain change, but subjectively they are not yet conscious of the need, not yet willing or determined to make the change. In such cases, we should wait patiently. We should not make the change until, through our work, most of the masses have become conscious of the need and are willing and determined to carry it out. Otherwise we shall isolate ourselves from the masses. . . . There are two principles here: one is the actual needs of the masses rather than what we fancy they need, and the other is the wishes of the masses, who must make up their own minds instead of our making up their minds for them." From the *Selected Works of Mao-Tse-Tung*, Vol. III. "The United Front in Cultural Work" (October 30, 1944) (Peking, 1967), pp. 186–187.

alongside the people for the recovery of the people's stolen humanity, not to "win the people over" to their side. Such a phrase does not belong in the vocabulary of revolutionary leaders, but in that of the oppressor. The revolutionary's role is to liberate, and be liberated, with the people—not to win them over.

In their political activity, the dominant elites utilize the banking concept to encourage passivity in the oppressed, corresponding with the latter's "submerged" state of consciousness, and take advantage of that passivity to "fill" that consciousness with slogans which create even more fear of freedom. This practice is incompatible with a truly liberating course of action, which, by presenting the oppressors' slogans as a problem, helps the oppressed to "eject" those slogans from within themselves. After all, the task of the humanists is surely not that of pitting their slogans against the slogans of the oppressors, with the oppressed as the testing ground, "housing" the slogans of first one group and then the other. On the contrary, the task of the humanists is to see that the oppressed become aware of the fact that as dual beings, "housing" the oppressors within themselves, they cannot be truly human.

This task implies that revolutionary leaders do not go to the people in order to bring them a message of "salvation," but in order to come to know through dialogue with them both their *objective situation* and their *awareness* of that situation—the various levels of perception of themselves and of the world in which and with which they exist. One cannot expect positive results from an educational or political action program which fails to respect the particular view of the world held by the people. Such a program constitutes cultural invasion,[11] good intentions notwithstanding.

The starting point for organizing the program content of education or political action must be the present, existential, concrete situation, reflecting the aspirations of the people. Utilizing certain basic contradictions, we must pose this existential, concrete, present situation to the people as a problem which challenges them and requires

---

[11] This point will be analyzed in detail in chapter 4.

a response—not just at the intellectual level, but at the level of action.[12]

We must never merely discourse on the present situation, must never provide the people with programs which have little or nothing to do with their own preoccupations, doubts, hopes, and fears— programs which at times in fact increase the fears of the oppressed consciousness. It is not our role to speak to the people about our own view of the world, nor to attempt to impose that view on them, but rather to dialogue with the people about their view and ours. We must realize that their view of the world, manifested variously in their action, reflects their *situation* in the world. Educational and political action which is not critically aware of this situation runs the risk either of "banking" or of preaching in the desert.

Often, educators and politicians speak and are not understood because their language is not attuned to the concrete situation of the people they address. Accordingly, their talk is just alienated and alienating rhetoric. The language of the educator or the politician (and it seems more and more clear that the latter must also become an educator, in the broadest sense of the word), like the language of the people, cannot exist without thought; and neither language nor thought can exist without a structure to which they refer. In order to communicate effectively, educator and politician must understand the structural conditions in which the thought and language of the people are dialectically framed.

It is to the reality which mediates men, and to the perception of that reality held by educators and people, that we must go to find the program content of education. The investigation of what I have termed the people's "thematic universe"[13]—the complex of their "generative themes"—inaugurates the dialogue of education as the practice of freedom. The methodology of that investigation must likewise be dialogical, affording the opportunity both to discover

---

[12] It is as self-contradictory for true humanists to use the banking method as it would be for rightists to engage in problem-posing education. (The latter are always consistent—they never use a problem-posing pedagogy.)

[13] The expression "meaningful thematics" is used with the same connotation.

generative themes and to stimulate people's awareness in regard to these themes. Consistent with the liberating purpose of dialogical education, the object of the investigation is not persons (as if they were anatomical fragments), but rather the thought-language with which men and women refer to reality, the levels at which they perceive that reality, and their view of the world, in which their generative themes are found.

Before describing a "generative theme" more precisely, which will also clarify what is meant by a "minimum thematic universe," it seems to me indispensable to present a few preliminary reflections. The concept of a generative theme is neither an arbitrary invention nor a working hypothesis to be proved. If it were a hypothesis to be proved, the initial investigation would seek not to ascertain the nature of the theme, but rather the very existence or non-existence of themes themselves. In that event, before attempting to understand the theme in its richness, its significance, its plurality, its transformations, and its historical composition, we would first have to verify whether or not it is an objective fact; only then could we proceed to apprehend it. Although an attitude of critical doubt is legitimate, it does appear possible to verify the reality of the generative theme—not only through one's own existential experience, but also through critical reflection on the human-world relationship and on the relationships between people implicit in the former.

This point deserves more attention. One may well remember—trite as it seems—that, of the uncompleted beings, man is the only one to treat not only his actions but his very self as the object of his reflection; this capacity distinguishes him from the animals, which are unable to separate themselves from their activity and thus are unable to reflect upon it. In this apparently superficial distinction lie the boundaries which delimit the action of each in his life space. Because the animals' activity is an extension of themselves, the results of that activity are also inseparable from themselves: animals can neither set objectives nor infuse their transformation of nature with any significance beyond itself. Moreover, the "decision" to perform this activity belongs not to them but to their species. Animals are, accordingly, fundamentally "beings in themselves."

Unable to decide for themselves, unable to objectify either themselves or their activity, lacking objectives which they themselves
have set, living "submerged" in a world to which they can give no
meaning, lacking a "tomorrow" and a "today" because they exist in
an overwhelming present, animals are ahistorical. Their ahistorical
life does not occur in the "world," taken in its strict meaning; for
the animal, the world does not constitute a "not-I" which could set
him apart as an "I." The human world, which is historical, serves as
a mere prop for the "being in itself." Animals are not challenged by
the configuration which confronts them; they are merely stimulated.
Their life is not one of risk-taking, for they are not aware of taking
risks. Risks are not challenges perceived upon reflection, but merely
"noted" by the signs which indicate them; they accordingly do not
require decision-making responses.

Consequently, animals cannot commit themselves. Their ahistorical condition does not permit them to "take on" life. Because
they do not "take it on," they cannot construct it; and if they do not
construct it, they cannot transform its configuration. Nor can they
know themselves to be destroyed by life, for they cannot expand
their "prop" world into a meaningful, symbolic world which includes
culture and history. As a result, animals do not "animalize" their
configuration in order to animalize themselves—nor do they "de-
animalize" themselves. Even in the forest, they remain "beings-in-
themselves," as animal-like there as in the zoo.

In contrast, the people—aware of their activity and the world in
which they are situated, acting in function of the objectives which
they propose, having the seat of their decisions located in themselves
and in their relations with the world and with others, infusing the
world with their creative presence by means of the transformation
they effect upon it—unlike animals, not only live but exist;[14] and
their existence is historical. Animals live out their lives on an atemp-
oral, flat, uniform "prop"; humans exist in a world which they are

---

[14] In the English language, the terms "live" and "exist" have assumed implications opposite to their etymological origins. As used here, "live" is the more basic
term, implying only survival; "exist" implies a deeper involvement in the process
of "becoming."

constantly re-creating and transforming. For animals, "here" is only a habitat with which they enter into contact; for people, "here" signifies not merely a physical space, but also an historical space.

Strictly speaking, "here," "now," "there," "tomorrow," and "yesterday" do not exist for the animal, whose life, lacking self-consciousness, is totally determined. Animals cannot surmount the limits imposed by the "here," the "now," or the "there."

Humans, however, because they are aware of themselves and thus of the world—because they are *conscious beings*—exist in a dialectical relationship between the determination of limits and their own freedom. As they separate themselves from the world, which they objectify, as they separate themselves from their own activity, as they locate the seat of their decisions in themselves and in their relations with the world and others, people overcome the situations which limit them: the "limit-situations."[15] Once perceived by individuals as fetters, as obstacles to their liberation, these situations stand out in relief from the background, revealing their true nature as concrete historical dimensions of a given reality. Men and women respond to the challenge with actions which Vieira Pinto calls "limit-acts": those directed at negating and overcoming, rather than passively accepting, the "given."

Thus, it is not the limit-situations in and of themselves which create a climate of hopelessness, but rather how they are perceived by women and men at a given historical moment: whether they appear as fetters or as insurmountable barriers. As critical perception is embodied in action, a climate of hope and confidence develops which leads men to attempt to overcome the limit-situations. This objective can be achieved only through action upon the con-

---

[15] Professor Alvaro Vieira Pinto analyzes with clarity the problem of "limit-situations," using the concept without the pessimistic aspect originally found in Jaspers. For Vieira Pinto, the "limit-situations" are not "the impassable boundaries where possibilities end, but the real boundaries where all possibilities begin"; they are not "the frontier which separates being from nothingness, but the frontier which separates being from nothingness but the frontier which separates being from being more." Alvaro Vieira Pinto, *Consciência e Realidade Nacional* (Rio de Janeiro, 1960), Vol. II, p. 284.

crete, historical reality in which limit-situations historically are found. As reality is transformed and these situations are superseded, new ones will appear, which in turn will evoke new limit-acts.

The prop world of animals contains no limit-situations, due to its ahistorical character. Similarly, animals lack the ability to exercise limit-acts, which require a decisive attitude towards the world: separation from and objectification of the world in order to transform it. Organically bound to their prop, animals do not distinguish between themselves and the world. Accordingly, animals are not limited by limit-situations—which are historical—but rather by the entire prop. And the appropriate role for animals is not to relate to their prop (in that event, the prop would be a world), but to adapt to it. Thus, when animals "produce" a nest, a hive, or a burrow, they are not creating products which result from "limit-acts," that is, transforming responses. Their productive activity is subordinated to the satisfaction of a physical necessity which is simply stimulating, rather than challenging. "An animal's product belongs immediately to its physical body, whilst man freely confronts his product."[16]

Only products which result from the activity of a being but do not belong to its physical body (though these products may bear its seal), can give a dimension of meaning to the context, which thus becomes a world. A being capable of such production (who thereby is necessarily aware of himself, is a "being for himself") could no longer *be* if she or he were not *in the process of being* in the world with which he or she relates; just as the world would no longer exist if this being did not exist.

The difference between animals—who (because their activity does not constitute limit-acts) cannot create products detached from themselves—and humankind—who through their action upon the world create the realm of culture and history—is that only the latter are beings of the praxis. Only human beings *are* praxis—the praxis which, as the reflection and action which truly transform reality, is

---

[16] Karl Marx, *Economic and Philosophical Manuscripts of 1844*, Dirk Struik, ed. (New York, 1964), p. 113.

the source of knowledge and creation. Animal activity, which occurs without a praxis, is not creative; people's transforming activity is.

It is as transforming and creative beings that humans, in their permanent relations with reality, produce not only material goods— tangible objects—but also social institutions, ideas, and concepts.[17] Through their continuing praxis, men and women simultaneously create history and become historical-social beings. Because—in contrast to animals—people can tri-dimensionalize time into the past, the present, and the future, their history, in function of their own creations, develops as a constant process of transformation within which epochal units materialize. These epochal units are not closed periods of time, static compartments within which people are confined. Were this the case, a fundamental condition of history—its continuity—would disappear. On the contrary, epochal units interrelate in the dynamics of historical continuity.[18]

An epoch is characterized by a complex of ideas, concepts, hopes, doubts, values, and challenges in dialectical interaction with their opposites, striving towards plenitude. The concrete representation of many of these ideas, values, concepts, and hopes, as well as the obstacles which impede the people's full humanization, constitute the themes of that epoch. These themes imply others which are opposing or even antithetical; they also indicate tasks to be carried out and fulfilled. Thus, historical themes are never isolated, independent, disconnected, or static; they are always interacting dialectically with their opposites. Nor can these themes be found anywhere except in the human-world relationship. The complex of interacting themes of an epoch constitutes its "thematic universe."

Confronted by this "universe of themes" in dialectical contradiction, persons take equally contradictory positions: some work to maintain the structures, others to change them. As antagonism deepens between themes which are the expression of reality, there

---

[17] Regarding this point, see Karel Kosik, *Dialética de lo Concreto* (Mexico, 1967).

[18] On the question of historical epochs, see Hans Freyer, *Teoría de la época atual* (Mexico).

is a tendency for the themes and for reality itself to be mythicized, establishing a climate of irrationality and sectarianism. This climate threatens to drain the themes of their deeper significance and to deprive them of their characteristically dynamic aspect. In such a situation, myth-creating irrationality itself becomes a fundamental theme. Its opposing theme, the critical and dynamic view of the world, strives to unveil reality, unmask its mythicization, and achieve a full realization of the human task: the permanent transformation of reality in favor of the liberation of people.

In the last analysis, the *themes*[19] both contain and are contained in *limit-situations;* the *tasks* they imply require *limit-acts.* When the themes are concealed by the limit-situations and thus are not clearly perceived, the corresponding tasks—people's responses in the form of historical action—can be neither authentically nor critically fulfilled. In this situation, humans are unable to transcend the limitsituations to discover that beyond these situations—and in contradiction to them—lies an *untested feasibility.*

In sum, limit-situations imply the existence of persons who are directly or indirectly served by these situations, and of those who are negated and curbed by them. Once the latter come to perceive these situations as the frontier between being and being more human, rather than the frontier between being and nothingness, they begin to direct their increasingly critical actions towards achieving the untested feasibility implicit in that perception. On the other hand, those who are served by the present limit-situation regard the untested feasibility as a threatening limit-situation which must not be allowed to materialize, and act to maintain the status quo. Consequently, liberating actions upon an historical milieu must correspond not only to the generative themes but to the way in which these themes are perceived. This requirement in turn implies another: the investigation of meaningful thematics.

---

[19] I have termed these themes "generative" because (however they are comprehended and whatever action they may evoke) they contain the possibility of unfolding into again as many themes, which in their turn call for new tasks to be fulfilled.

Generative themes can be located in concentric circles, moving from the general to the particular. The broadest epochal unit, which includes a diversified range of units and sub-units—continental, regional, national, and so forth—contains themes of a universal character. I consider the fundamental theme of our epoch to be that of *domination*—which implies its opposite, the theme of *liberation,* as the objective to be achieved. It is this tormenting theme which gives our epoch the anthropological character mentioned earlier. In order to achieve humanization, which presupposes the elimination of dehumanizing oppression, it is absolutely necessary to surmount the limit-situations in which people are reduced to things.

Within the smaller circles, we find themes and limit-situations characteristic of societies (on the same continent or on different continents) which through these themes and limit-situations share historical similarities. For example, underdevelopment, which cannot be understood apart from the relationship of dependency, represents a limit-situation characteristic of societies of the Third World. The task implied by this limit-situation is to overcome the contradictory relation of these "object"-societies to the metropolitan societies; this task constitutes the untested feasibility for the Third World.

Any given society within the broader epochal unit contains, in addition to the universal, continental, or historically similar themes, its own particular themes, its own limit-situations. Within yet smaller circles, thematic diversifications can be found within the same society, divided into areas and sub-areas, all of which are related to the societal whole. These constitute epochal sub-units. For example, within the same national unit one can find the contradiction of the "coexistence of the non-contemporaneous."

Within these sub-units, national themes may or may not be perceived in their true significance. They may simply be *felt*— sometimes not even that. But the nonexistence of themes within the sub-units is absolutely impossible. The fact that individuals in a certain area do not perceive a generative theme, or perceive it in a distorted way, may only reveal a limit-situation of oppression in which people are still submerged.

In general, a dominated consciousness which has not yet perceived a limit-situation in its totality apprehends only its epiphenomena and transfers to the latter the inhibiting force which is the property of the limit-situation.[20] This fact is of great importance for the investigation of generative themes. When people lack a critical understanding of their reality, apprehending it in fragments which they do not perceive as interacting constituent elements of the whole, they cannot truly know that reality. To truly know it, they would have to reverse their starting point: they would need to have a total vision of the context in order subsequently to separate and isolate its constituent elements and by means of this analysis achieve a clearer perception of the whole.

Equally appropriate for the methodology of thematic investigation and for problem-posing education is this effort to present significant dimensions of an individual's contextual reality, the analysis of which will make it possible for him to recognize the interaction of the various components. Meanwhile, the significant dimensions, which in their turn are constituted of parts in interaction, should be perceived as dimensions of total reality. In this way, a critical analysis of a significant existential dimension makes possible a new, critical attitude towards the limit-situations. The perception and comprehension of reality are rectified and acquire new depth. When carried out with a methodology of *conscientização* the investigation of the generative theme contained in the minimum thematic universe (the generative themes in interaction) thus introduces or begins to introduce women and men to a critical form of thinking about their world.

---

[20] Individuals of the middle class often demonstrate this type of behavior, although in a different way from the peasant. Their fear of freedom leads them to erect defense mechanisms and rationalizations which conceal the fundamental, emphasize the fortuitous, and deny concrete reality. In the face of a problem whose analysis would lead to the uncomfortable perception of a limit-situation, their tendency is to remain on the periphery of the discussion and resist any attempt to reach the heart of the question. They are even annoyed when someone points out a fundamental proposition which explains the fortuitous or secondary matters to which they had been assigning primary importance.

In the event, however, that human beings perceive reality as dense, impenetrable, and enveloping, it is indispensable to proceed with the investigation by means of abstraction. This method does not involve reducing the concrete to the abstract (which would signify the negation of its dialectical nature), but rather maintaining both elements as opposites which interrelate dialectically in the act of reflection. This dialectical movement of thought is exemplified perfectly in the analysis of a concrete existential, "coded" situation.[21] Its "decoding" requires moving from the abstract to the concrete; this requires moving from the part to the whole and then returning to the parts; this in turn requires that the Subject recognize himself in the object (the coded concrete existential situation) and recognize the object as a situation in which he finds himself, together with other Subjects. If the decoding is well done, this movement of flux and reflux from the abstrct to the concrete which occurs in the analysis of a coded situation leads to the supersedence of the abstraction *by* the critical perception of the concrete, which has already ceased to be a dense, impenetrable reality.

When an individual is presented with a coded existential situation (a sketch or photograph which leads by abstraction to the concreteness of existential reality), his tendency is to "split" that coded situation. In the process of decoding, this separation corresponds to the stage we call the "description of the situation," and facilitates the discovery of the interaction among the parts of the disjoined whole. This whole (the coded situation), which previously had been only diffusely apprehended, begins to acquire meaning as thought flows back to it from the various dimensions. Since; however, the coding is the representation of an existential situation, the decoder tends to take the step from the representation to the very concrete situation in which and with which she finds herself. It is thus possible to explain conceptually why individuals begin to behave differently with regard to objective reality, once that reality has ceased to look

---

[21] The coding of an existential situation is the representation of that situation, showing some of its constituent elements in interaction. Decoding is the critical analysis of the coded situation.

like a blind alley and has taken on its true aspect: a challenge which human beings must meet.

In all the stages of decoding, people exteriorize their view of the world. And in the way they think about and face the world—fatalistically, dynamically, or statically—their generative themes may be found. A group which does not concretely express a generative thematics—a fact which might appear to imply the nonexistence of themes—is, on the contrary, suggesting a very dramatic theme: *the theme of silence.* The theme of silence suggests a structure of mutism in face of the overwhelming force of the limit-situations.

I must re-emphasize that the generative theme cannot be found in people, divorced from reality; nor yet in reality, divorced from people; much less in "no man's land." It can only be apprehended in the human-world relationship. To investigate the generative theme is to investigate people's thinking about reality and people's action upon reality, which is their praxis. For precisely this reason, the methodology proposed requires that the investigators and the people (who would normally be considered objects of that investigation) should act as *co-investigators.* The more active an attitude men and women take in regard to the exploration of their thematics, the more they deepen their critical awareness of reality and, in spelling out those thematics, take possession of that reality.

Some may think it inadvisable to include the people as investigators in the search for their own meaningful thematics: that their intrusive influence (n.b., the "intrusion" of those who are most interested—or ought to be—in their own education) will "adulterate" the findings and thereby sacrifice the objectivity of the investigation. This view mistakenly presupposes that themes exist, in their original objective purity, outside people—as if themes were *things.* Actually, themes exist in people in their relations with the world, with reference to concrete facts. The same objective fact could evoke different complexes of generative themes in different epochal sub-units. There is, therefore, a relation between the given objective fact, the perception women and men have of this fact, and the generative themes.

A meaningful thematics is expressed by people, and a given moment of expression will differ from an earlier moment, if they have changed their perception of the objective facts to which the themes refer. From the investigator's point of view, the important thing is to detect the starting point at which the people visualize the "given" and to verify whether or not during the process of investigation any transformation has occurred in their way of perceiving reality. (Objective reality, of course, remains unchanged. If the perception of that reality changes in the course of the investigation, that fact does not impair the validity of the investigation.)

We must realize that the aspirations, the motives, and the objectives implicit in the meaningful thematics are *human* aspirations, motives, and objectives. They do not exist "out there" somewhere, as static entities; *they are occurring*. They are as historical as human beings themselves; consequently, they cannot be apprehended apart from them. To apprehend these themes and to understand them is to understand both the people who embody them and the reality to which they refer. But—precisely because it is not possible to understand these themes apart from people—it is necessary that those concerned understand them as well. Thematic investigation thus becomes a common striving towards awareness of reality and towards self-awareness, which makes this investigation a starting point for the educational process or for cultural action of a liberating character.

The real danger of the investigation is not that the supposed objects of the investigation, discovering themselves to be co-investigators, might "adulterate" the analytical results. On the contrary, the danger lies in the risk of shifting the focus of the investigation from the meaningful themes to the people themselves, thereby treating the people as objects of the investigation. Since this investigation is to serve as a basis for developing an educational program in which teacher-student and students-teachers combine their cognitions of the same object, the investigation itself must likewise be based on reciprocity of action.

Thematic investigation, which occurs in the realm of the human, cannot be reduced to a mechanical act. As a process of search, of knowledge, and thus of creation, it requires the investigators to discover the interpenetration of problems, in the linking of meaningful themes. The investigation will be most educational when it is most critical, and most critical when it avoids the narrow outlines of partial or "focalized" views of reality, and sticks to the comprehension of *total* reality. Thus, the process of searching for the meaningful thematics should include a concern for the links between themes, a concern to pose these themes as problems, and a concern for their historical-cultural context.

Just as the educator may not elaborate a program to present *to* the people, neither may the investigator elaborate "itineraries" for researching the thematic universe, starting from points which *he* has predetermined. Both education and the investigation designed to support it must be "sympathetic" activities, in the etymological sense of the word. That is, they must consist of communication and of the common experience of a reality perceived in the complexity of its constant "becoming."

The investigator who, in the name of scientific objectivity, transforms the organic into something inorganic, what is becoming into what is, life into death, is a person who fears change. He or she sees in change (which is not denied, but neither is it desired) not a sign of life, but a sign of death and decay. He or she does want to study change—but in order to stop it, not in order to stimulate or deepen it. However, in seeing change as a sign of death and in making people the passive objects of investigation in order to arrive at rigid models, one betrays their own character as a killer of life.

I repeat: the investigation of thematics involves the investigation of the people's thinking—thinking which occurs only in and among people together seeking out reality. I cannot think *for others* or *without others*, nor can others think *for me*. Even if the people's thinking is superstitious or naive, it is only as they rethink their assumptions in action that they can change. Producing and acting upon their own ideas—not consuming those of others—must constitute that process.

People, as beings "in a situation," find themselves rooted in temporal-spatial conditions which mark them and which they also mark. They will tend to reflect on their own "situationality" to the extent that they are challenged by it to act upon it. Human beings *are* because they *are in* a situation. And they *will be more* the more they not only critically reflect upon their existence but critically act upon it.

Reflection upon situationality is reflection about the very condition of existence: critical thinking by means of which people discover each other to be "in a situation." Only as this situation ceases to present itself as a dense, enveloping reality or a tormenting blind alley, and they can come to perceive it as an objective-problematic situation—only then can commitment exist. Humankind *emerge* from their *submersion* and acquire the ability to *intervene* in reality as it is unveiled. *Intervention* in reality—historical awareness itself—thus represents a step forward from *emergence,* and results from the *conscientização* of the situation. *Conscientização* is the deepening of the attitude of awareness characteristic of all emergence.

Every thematic investigation which deepens historical awareness is thus really educational, while all authentic education investigates thinking. The more educators and the people investigate the people's thinking, and are thus jointly educated, the more they continue to investigate. Education and thematic investigation, in the problem-posing concept of education, are simply different moments of the same process.

In contrast with the antidialogical and non-communicative "deposits" of the banking method of education, the program content of the problem-posing method—dialogical par excellence—is constituted and organized by the students' view of the world, where their own generative themes are found. The content thus constantly expands and renews itself. The task of the dialogical teacher in an interdisciplinary team working on the thematic universe revealed by their investigation is to "re-present" that universe to the people from whom she or he first received it—and "re-present" it not as a lecture, but as a problem.

Let us say, for example, that a group has the responsibility of coordinating a plan for adult education in a peasant area with a high percentage of illiteracy. The plan includes a literacy campaign and a post-literacy phase. During the former stage, problem-posing education seeks out and investigates the "generative word"; in the post-literacy stage, it seeks out and investigates the "generative theme."

Let us here, however, consider only the investigation of the generative themes or the meaningful thematics.[22] Once the investigators have determined the area in which they will work and have acquired a preliminary acquaintance with the area through secondary sources, they initiate the first stage of the investigation. This beginning (like any beginning in any human activity) involves difficulties and risks which are to a certain point normal, although they are not always evident in the first contact with the individuals of the area. In this first contact, the investigators need to get a significant number of persons to agree to an informal meeting during which they can talk about the objectives of their presence in the area. In this meeting they explain the reason for the investigation, how it is to be carried out, and to what use it will be put; they further explain that the investigation will be impossible without a relation of mutual understanding and trust. If the participants agree both to the investigation and to the subsequent process,[23] the investigators should call for volunteers among the participants to serve as assistants. These volunteers will gather a series of necessary data about the life of the area. Of even greater importance, however, is the active presence of these volunteers in the investigation.

Meanwhile, the investigators begin their own visits to the area, never forcing themselves, but acting as sympathetic observers with an attitude of *understanding* towards what they see. While it is normal for investigators to come to the area with values which influ-

---

[22] Regarding the investigation and use of "generative words," see my *Educação como Prática da Liberdade*.

[23] According to the Brazilian sociologist Maria Edy Ferreira (in an unpublished work), thematic investigation is only justified to the extent that it returns to the people what truly belongs to them; to the extent that it represents, not an attempt to learn about the people, but to come to know with them the reality which challenges them.

ence their perceptions, this does not mean that they may transform the thematic investigation into a means of imposing these values. The only dimension of these values which it is hoped the people whose thematics are being investigated will come to share (it is presumed that the investigators possess this quality) is a critical perception of the world, which implies a correct method of approaching reality in order to unveil it. And critical perception cannot be imposed. Thus, from the very beginning, thematic investigation is expressed as an educational pursuit, as cultural action.

During their visits, the investigators set their critical "aim" on the area under study, as if it were for them an enormous, unique, living "code" to be deciphered. They regard the area as a totality, and visit upon visit attempt to "split" it by analyzing the partial dimensions which impress them. Through this process they expand their understanding of how the various parts interact, which will later help them penetrate the totality itself.

During this decoding stage, the investigators observe certain *moments* of the life of the area—sometimes directly, sometimes by means of informal conversations with the inhabitants. They register everything in their notebooks, including apparently unimportant items: the way the people talk, their style of life, their behavior at church and at work. They record the idiom of the people: their expressions, their vocabulary, and their syntax (not their incorrect pronunciation, but rather the way they construct their thought).[24]

It is essential that the investigators observe the area under varying circumstances: labor in the fields, meetings of a local association (noting the behavior of the participants, the language used, and the

---

[24] The Brazilian novelist Guimaraẽs Rosa is a brilliant example of how a writer can capture authentically, not the pronunciation or the grammatical corruptions of the people, but their syntax: the very structure of their thought. Indeed (and this is not to disparage his exceptional value as a writer), Guimaraes Rosa was the investigator par excellence of the "meaningful thematics" of the inhabitants of the Brazilian hinterland. Professor Paulo de Tarso is currently preparing an essay which analyzes this little-considered aspect of the work of the author of *Grande Sertão— Veredas* [in English translation: *The Devil to Pay in the Backlands* (New York, 1963)].

relations between the officers and the members), the role played by women and by young people, leisure hours, games and sports, conversations with people in their homes (noting examples of husband-wife and parent-child relationships). No activity must escape the attention of the investigators during the initial survey of the area.

After each observation visit, the investigator should draw up a brief report to be discussed by the entire team, in order to evaluate the preliminary findings of both the professional investigators and the local assistants. To facilitate the participation of the assistants, the evaluation meetings should be held in the area itself.

The evaluation meetings represent a second stage in the decoding of the unique living code. As each person, in his decoding essay, relates how he perceived or felt a certain occurrence or situation, his exposition challenges all the other decoders by re-presenting to them the same reality upon which they have themselves been intent. At this moment they "re-consider," through the "considerations" of others, their own previous "consideration." Thus the analysis of reality made by each individual decoder sends them all back, dialogically, to the disjoined whole which once more becomes a totality evoking a new analysis by the investigators, following which a new evaluative and critical meeting will be held. Representatives of the inhabitants participate in all activities as members of the investigating team.

The more the group divide and reintegrate the whole, the more closely they approach the nuclei of the principal and secondary contradictions which involve the inhabitants of the area. By locating these nuclei of contradictions, the investigators might even at this stage be able to organize the program content of their educational action. Indeed, if the content reflected these contradictions, it would undoubtedly contain the meaningful thematics of the area. And one can safely affirm that action based on these observations would be much more likely to succeed than that based on "decisions from the top." The investigators should not, however, be tempted by this possibility. The basic thing, starting from the initial perception of these nuclei of contradictions (which include the principal contradiction of society as a larger epochal unit) is to study the inhabitants' level of awareness of these contradictions.

Intrinsically, these contradictions constitute limit-situations, involve themes, and indicate tasks. If individuals are caught up in and are unable to separate themselves from these limit-situations, their theme in reference to these situations is *fatalism,* and the task implied by the theme is *the lack of a task.* Thus, although the limit-situations are objective realities which call forth needs in individuals, one must investigate with these individuals their level of awareness of these situations.

A limit-situation as a concrete reality can call forth from persons in different areas (and even in sub-areas of the same area) quite opposite themes and tasks. Thus, the basic concern of the investigators should be to concentrate on the knowledge of what Goldman calls "real consciousness" and the "potential consciousness."

> Real consciousness [is] the result of the multiple obstacles and deviations that the different factors of empirical reality put into opposition and submit for realization by [the] potential consciousness.[25]

Real consciousness implies the impossibility of perceiving the "untested feasibility" which lies beyond the limit-situations. But whereas the untested feasibility cannot be achieved at the level of "real [or present] consciousness," it can be realized through "testing action" which reveals its hitherto unperceived viability. The untested feasibility and real consciousness are related, as are testing action and potential consciousness. Goldman's concept of "potential consciousness" is similar to what Nicolaï terms "unperceived praticable solutions"[26] (our "untested feasibility"), in contrast to "perceived practicable solutions" and "presently practiced solutions," which

---

[25] Lucien Goldman, *The Human Sciences and Philosophy* (London, 1969), p. 118.
[26] See André Nicolaï, *Comportment Économique et Structures Sociales* (Paris, 1960).

correspond to Goldman's "real consciousness." Accordingly, the fact that the investigators may in the first stage of the investigation approximately apprehend the complex of contradictions does not authorize them to begin to structure the program content of educational action. This perception of reality is still their own, not that of the people.

It is with the apprehension of the complex of contradictions that the second stage of the investigation begins. Always acting as a team, the investigators will select some of these contradictions to develop the codifications to be used in the thematic investigation. Since the codifications (sketches or photographs)[27] are the *objects* which mediate the decoders in their critical analysis, the preparation of these codifications must be guided by certain principles other than the usual ones for making visual aids.

The first requirement is that these codifications must necessarily represent situations familiar to the individuals whose thematics are being examined, so that they can easily recognize the situations (and thus their own relation to them). It is inadmissible (whether during the process of investigation or in the following stage, when the meaningful thematics are presented as program content) to present pictures of reality unfamiliar to the participants. The latter procedure (although dialectical, because individuals analyzing an unfamiliar reality could compare it with their own and discover the limitations of each) cannot precede the more basic one dictated by the participants' state of submersion, that is, the process in which individuals analyzing their own reality become aware of their prior, distorted perceptions and thereby come to have a new perception of that reality.

An equally fundamental requirement for the preparation of the codifications is that their thematic nucleus be neither overly explicit nor overly enigmatic. The former may degenerate into mere propa-

---

[27] The codifications may also be oral. In this case they consist of a few words presenting an existential problem, followed by decoding. The team of the *Instituto de Desarrollo Agropecuario* (Institute for Agrarian Development) in Chile has used this method successfully in thematic investigations.

ganda, with no real decoding to be done beyond stating the obviously predetermined content. The latter runs the risk of appearing to be a puzzle or a guessing game. Since they represent existential situations, the codifications should be simple in their complexity and offer various decoding possibilities in order to avoid the brainwashing tendencies of propaganda. Codifications are not slogans; they are cognizable objects, challenges towards which the critical reflection of the decoders should be directed.

In order to offer various possibilities of analysis in the decoding process, the codifications should be organized as a "thematic fan." As the decoders reflect on the codifications, the codifications should open up in the direction of other themes. This opening up (which does not occur if the thematic content is either too explicit or too enigmatic) is indispensable to the perception of the dialectical relations which exist between the themes and their opposites. Accordingly, the codifications reflecting an existential situation must objectively constitute a totality. Its elements must interact in the makeup of the whole.

In the process of decoding, the participants externalize their thematics and thereby make explicit their "real consciousness" of the world. As they do this, they begin to see how they themselves acted while actually experiencing the situation they are now analyzing, and thus reach a "perception of their previous perception." By achieving this awareness, they come to perceive reality differently; by broadening the horizon of their perception, they discover more easily in their "background awareness" the dialectical relations between the two dimensions of reality.

By stimulating "perception of the previous perception" and "knowledge of the previous knowledge," decoding stimulates the appearance of a new perception and the development of new knowledge. The new perception and knowledge are systematically continued with the inauguration of the educational plan, which transforms the untested feasibility into testing action, as potential consciousness supersedes real consciousness.

Preparing the codifications further requires that insofar as possible they should represent contradictions "inclusive" of others which constitute the system of contradictions of the area under study.[28] As each of these "inclusive" codifications is prepared, the other contradictions "contained" therein should also be codified. The decoding of the former will be dialectically clarified by the decoding of the latter.

In this connection, a very valuable contribution to our method has been made by Gabriel Bode, a young Chilean civil servant in one of the most significant Chilean governmental institutions: the *Instituto de Desarrollo Agropecuario* (INDAP).[29] During his use of this method in the post-literacy stage, Bode observed that the peasants became interested in the discussion only when the codification related directly to their felt needs. Any deviation in the codification, as well as any attempt by the educator to guide the decoding discussion into other areas, produced silence and indifference. On the other hand, he observed that even when the codification[30] centered on their felt needs the peasants could not manage to concentrate systematically on the discussion, which often digressed to the point of never reaching a synthesis. Also, they almost never perceived the relationship of their felt needs to the direct and indirect causes of these needs. One might say that they failed to perceive the untested feasibility lying beyond the limit-situations which engendered their needs.

Bode then decided to experiment with the simultaneous projection of different situations; in this technique lies the value of his contribution. Initially, he projects a very simple codification of an existential situation. He terms his first codification "essential"; it represents the basic nucleus and opens up into a thematic fan extending to "auxiliary" codifications. After the essential codification is decoded, the educator maintains its projected image as a reference

---

[28] This recommendation is made by José Luis Fiori, in an unpublished manuscript.

[29] Until recently, INDAP was directed by the economist and authentic humanist Jacques Chonchol.

[30] These codifications were not "inclusive," in Fiori's definition.

for the participants and successively projects alongside it the auxiliary codifications. By means of the latter, which are directly related to the essential codification, he sustains the vivid interest of the participants, who are thereby enabled to reach a synthesis.

The great achievement of Gabriel Bode is that, by means of the dialectics between the essential and the auxiliary codifications, he has managed to communicate to the participants a sense of *totality.* Individuals who were *submerged* in reality, merely *feeling* their needs, *emerge* from reality and perceive the *causes* of their needs. In this way, they can go beyond the level of real consciousness to that of potential consciousness much more rapidly.

Once the codifications have been prepared and all their possible thematic facets have been studied by the interdisciplinary team, the investigators begin the third stage of the investigation by returning to the area to initiate decoding dialogues in the "thematic investigation circles."[31] These discussions, which decode the material prepared in the preceding stage, are taped for subsequent analysis by the interdisciplinary team.[32] In addition to the investigator acting as decoding co-ordinator, two other specialists—a psychologist and a sociologist—attend the meetings. Their task is to note and record the significant (and apparently insignificant) reactions of the decoders.

During the decoding process, the co-ordinator must not only lis-

---

[31] Each "investigation circle" should have a maximum of twenty persons. There should be as many circles as necessary to involve, as participants, ten percent of the area or sub-area being studied.

[32] These subsequent meetings of analysis should include the volunteers from the area who assisted in the investigation, and some participants of the "thematic investigation circles." Their contribution is both a right to which they are entitled and an indispensable aid to the analysis of the specialists. As co-investigators of the specialists, they will rectify and/or ratify the interpretations the latter make of the findings. From the methodological point of view, their participation gives the investigation (which from the beginning is based on a "sympathetic" relationship) an additional safeguard: the critical presence of representatives of the people from the beginning until the final phase, that of thematic analysis, continued in the organization of the program content of educational action as liberating cultural action.

ten to the individuals but must challenge them, posing as problems both the codified existential situation and their own answers. Due to the cathartic force of the methodology, the participants of the thematic investigation circles externalize a series of sentiments and opinions about themselves, the world, and others, that perhaps they would not express under different circumstances.

In one of the thematic investigations[33] carried out in Santiago, a group of tenement residents discussed a scene showing a drunken man walking on the street and three young men conversing on the corner. The group participants commented that "the only one there who is productive and useful to his country is the souse who is returning home after working all day for low wages and who is worried about his family because he can't take care of their needs. He is the only worker. He is a decent worker and a souse like us."

The investigator[34] had intended to study aspects of alcoholism. He probably would not have elicited the above responses if he had presented the participants with a questionnaire he had elaborated himself. If asked directly, they might even have denied ever taking a drink themselves. But in their comments on the codification of an existential situation they could recognize, and in which they could recognize themselves, they said what they really felt.

There are two important aspects to these declarations. On the one hand, they verbalize the connection between earning low wages, feeling exploited, and getting drunk—getting drunk as a flight from reality, as an attempt to overcome the frustration of inaction, as an ultimately self-destructive solution. On the other hand, they manifest the need to rate the drunkard highly. He is the "only one useful to his country, because he works, while the others only gab." After praising the drunkard, the participants then identify themselves with him, as workers who also drink—"decent workers."

In contrast, imagine the failure of a moralistic educator,[35] sermoniz-

---

[33] This particular investigation was, unfortunately, not completed.
[34] The psychiatrist Patricio Lopes, whose work is described in *Educação como Prática da Liberdade*.
[35] See Niebuhr, *op cit.*

ing against alcoholism and presenting as an example of virtue something which for these men is not a manifestation of virtue. In this and in other cases, the only sound procedure is the *conscientização* of the situation, which should be attempted from the start of the thematic investigation. (Obviously, *conscientização* does not stop at the level of mere subjective perception of a situation, but through action prepares men for the struggle against the obstacles to their humanization.)

In another experience, this time with peasants, I observed that the unchanging motif during an entire discussion of a situation depicting work in the fields was the demand for an increase in wages and the necessity of joining together to create a union to obtain this particular demand. Three situations were discussed during the session, and the motif was always the same.

Now imagine an educator who has organized *his* educational program for these men, consisting of reading "wholesome" texts in which one learns that "the water is in the well." But precisely this type of thing happens all the time in both education and politics, because it is not realized that the dialogical nature of education begins with thematic investigation.

Once the decoding in the circles has been completed, the last stage of the investigation begins, as the investigators undertake a systematic interdisciplinary study of their findings. Listening to the tapes recorded during the decoding sessions and studying the notes taken by the psychologists and the sociologist, the investigators begin to list the themes explicit or implicit in the affirmations made during the sessions. These themes should be classified according to the various social sciences. Classification does not mean that when the program is elaborated the themes will be seen as belonging to isolated categories, but only that a theme is viewed in a specific manner by each of the social sciences to which it is related. The theme of development, for example, is especially appropriate to the field of economics, but not exclusively so. This theme would also be focalized by sociology, anthropology, and social psychology (fields concerned with cultural change and with the modification of attitudes and values—questions which are equally relevant to a philoso-phy of development). It would be focalized by political science (a field concerned with the decisions which involve development), by education, and so forth. In this way, the themes which characterize a totality will never be approached rigidly. It would indeed be a pity if the themes, after being investigated in the richness of their interpenetration with other aspects of reality, were subsequently to be handled in such a way as to sacrifice their richness (and hence their force) to the strictures of specialties.

Once the thematic demarcation is completed, each specialist pre-sents to the interdisciplinary team a project for the "breakdown" of his theme. In breaking down the theme, the specialist looks for the fundamental nuclei which, comprising learning units and establish-ing a sequence, give a general view of the theme. As each specific project is discussed, the other specialists make suggestions. These may be incorporated into the project and/or may be included in the brief essays to be written on the theme, These essays, to which bibliographic suggestions are annexed, are valuable aids in training the teacher-students who will work in the "culture circles."

During this effort to break down the meaningful thematics, the team will recognize the need to include some fundamental themes which were not directly suggested by the people during the preced-ing investigation. The introduction of these themes has proved to be necessary, and also corresponds to the dialogical character of education. If educational programming is dialogical, the teacher-students also have the right to participate by including themes not previously suggested. I call the latter type of theme "hinged themes," due to their function. They may either facilitate the con-nection between two themes in the program unit, filling a possible gap between the two; or they may illustrate the relations between the general program content and the view of the world held by the people. Hence, one of these themes may be located at the beginning of thematic units.

The anthropological concept of culture is one of these hinged themes. It clarifies the role of people in the world and with the world as transforming rather than adaptive beings.[36]

Once the breakdown of the thematics is completed,[37] there follows the stage of its "codification": choosing the best channel of communication for each theme and its representation. A codification may be simple or compound. The former utilizes either the visual (pictorial or graphic), the tactile, or the auditive channel; the latter utilizes various channels.[38] The selection of the pictorial or graphic channel depends not only on the material to be codified, but also on whether or not the individuals with whom one wishes to communicate are literate.

After the thematics has been codified, the didactic material (photographs, slides, film strips, posters, reading texts, and so forth) is prepared. The team may propose some themes or aspects of some themes to outside specialists as topics for recorded interviews.

Let us take the theme of development as an example. The team

---

[36] With regard to the importance of the anthropological analysis of culture, see *Educação como Prática da Liberdade.*

[37] Note that the entire program is a totality made up of interrelated units which in themselves are also totalities.

The themes are totalities in themselves but are also elements which in interaction constitute the thematic units of the entire program.

The thematic breakdown splits the total themes in search of their fundamental nuclei, which are the partial elements.

The codification process attempts to re-totalize the disjoined theme in the representation of existential situations.

In decoding, individuals split the codification to apprehend its implicit theme or themes. The dialectical decoding process does not end there, but is completed in the re-totalization of the disjoined whole which is thus more clearly understood (as are also its relations to other codified situations, all of which represent existential situations).

[38] CODIFICATION
    a) Simple:
        visual channel
          pictorial
          graphic
        tactile channel
        auditive channel
    b) Compound: simultaneity of channels

approaches two or more economists of varying schools of thought, tells them about the program, and invites them to contribute an interview on the subject in language comprehensible to the audience. If the specialists accept, an interview of fifteen to twenty minutes is taped. A photograph may be taken of each specialist while he is speaking.

When the taped interview is presented to the culture circle, an introductory statement indicates who each speaker is, what she or he has written, done, and doing now; meanwhile, the speaker's photograph is projected on a screen. If, for instance, the speaker is a university professor, the introduction could include a discussion regarding what the participants think of universities and what they expect of them. The group has already been told that the recorded interview will be followed by a discussion of its contents (which function as an auditive codification). The team subsequently reports to the specialist the reaction of the participants during the discussion. This technique links intellectuals, often well-intentioned but not infrequently alienated from the reality of the people, to that reality. It also gives the people an opportunity to hear and criticize the thought of intellectuals.

Some themes or nuclei may be presented by means of brief dramatizations, containing the theme only—no "solutions"! The dramatization acts as a codification, as a problem-posing situation to be discussed.

Another didactic resource—as long as it is carried out within a problem-posing rather than a banking approach to education—is the reading and discussion of magazine articles, newspapers, and book chapters (beginning with passages). As in the case of the recorded interviews, the author is introduced before the group begins, and the contents are discussed afterward.

Along the same lines, it is indispensable to analyze the contents of newspaper editorials following any given event: "Why do different newspapers have such different interpretations of the same fact?" This practice helps develop a sense of criticism, so that people will react to newspapers or news broadcasts not as passive objects of the "communiqués" directed at them, but rather as consciousnesses seeking to be free.

With all the didactic material prepared, to which should be added small introductory manuals, the team of educators is ready to represent to the people their own thematics, in systematized and amplified form. The thematics which have come from the people return to them—not as contents to be deposited, but as problems to be solved.

The first task of the basic-education teachers is to present the general program of the educational campaign. The people will find themselves in this program; it will not seem strange to them, since it originated with them. The educators will also explain (based on the dialogical character of education) the presence in the program of the hinged themes, and their significance.

If the educators lack sufficient funds to carry out the preliminary thematic investigation as described above, they can—with a minimum knowledge of the situation—select some basic themes to serve as "codifications to be investigated." Accordingly, they can begin with introductory themes and simultaneously initiate further thematic investigation.

One of these basic themes (and one which I consider central and indispensable) is the anthropological concept of culture. Whether men and women are peasants or urban workers, learning to read or enrolled in a post-literacy program, the starting point of their search to know more (in the instrumental meaning of the term) is the debate of the concept. As they discuss the world of culture, they express their level of awareness of reality, in which various themes are implicit. Their discussion touches upon other aspects of reality, which comes to be perceived in an increasingly critical manner. These aspects in turn involve many other themes.

With the experience now behind me, I can affirm that the concept of culture, discussed imaginatively in all or most of its dimensions, can provide various aspects of an educational program. In addition, after several days of dialogue with the culture circle participants, the educators can ask the participants directly: "What other themes or subjects could we discuss besides these?" As each person replies, the answer is noted down and is immediately proposed to the group as a problem.

One of the group members may say, for example: "I'd like to talk abut nationalism." "Very well," says the educator, noting down the suggestion, and adds: "What does nationalism mean? Why is a discussion about nationalism of any interest to us?" My experience shows that when a suggestion is posed as a problem to the group, new themes appear. If, in an area where (for example) thirty culture circles meet on the same night, all the "co-ordinators" (educators) proceed in this fashion, the central team will have a rich variety of thematic material for study.

The important thing, from the point of view of libertarian education, is for the people to come to feel like masters of their thinking by discussing the thinking and views of the world explicitly or implicitly manifest in their own suggestions and those of their comrades. Because this view of education starts with the conviction that it cannot present its own program but must search for this program dialogically with the people, it serves to introduce the pedagogy of the oppressed, in the elaboration of which the oppressed must participate.

# CHAPTER

# 4

This chapter, which analyses the theories of cultural action which develop from antidialogical and dialogical matrices, will make frequent reference to points presented in the previous chapters, either to expand these points or to clarify new affirmations.

I shall start by reaffirming that humankind, as beings of the *praxis,* differ from animals, which are beings of pure activity. Animals do not consider the world; they are immersed in it. In contrast, human beings emerge from the world, objectify it, and in so doing can understand it and transform it with their labor.

Animals, which do not labor, live in a setting which they cannot transcend. Hence, each animal species lives in the context appropriate to it, and these contexts, while open to humans, cannot communicate among themselves.

But human activity consists of action and reflection: it is praxis; it is transformation of the world. And as praxis, it requires theory to illuminate it. Human activity is theory and practice; it is reflection and action. It cannot, as I stressed in chapter 2, be reduced to either verbalism or activism.

Lenin's famous statement: "Without a revolutionary theory there can be no revolutionary movement"[1] means that a revolution is

---
[1] Vladimir Lenin, "What is to be Done," in *Essential Works of Lenin,* Henry M. Christman, ed. (New York, 1966), p. 69.

achieved with neither verbalism nor activism, but rather with praxis, that is, with *reflection* and *action* directed at the structures to be transformed. The revolutionary effort to transform these structures radically cannot designate its leaders as its *thinkers* and the oppressed as mere *doers*.

If true commitment to the people, involving the transformation of the reality by which they are oppressed, requires a theory of transforming action, this theory cannot fail to assign the people a fundamental role in the transformation process. The leaders cannot treat the oppressed as mere activists to be denied the opportunity of reflection and allowed merely the illusion of acting, whereas in fact they would continue to be manipulated—and in this case by the presumed foes of manipulation.

The leaders do bear the responsibility for coordination and, at times, direction—but leaders who deny praxis to the oppressed thereby invalidate their own praxis. By imposing their word on others, they falsify that word and establish a contradiction between their methods and their objectives. If they are truly committed to liberation, their action and reflection cannot proceed without the action and reflection of others.

Revolutionary praxis must stand opposed to the praxis of the dominant elites, for they are by nature antithetical. Revolutionary praxis cannot tolerate an absurd dichotomy in which the praxis of the people is merely that of following the leaders' decisions—a di chotomy reflecting the prescriptive methods of the dominant elites. Revolutionary praxis is a unity, and the leaders cannot treat the oppressed as their possession.

Manipulation, sloganizing, "depositing," regimentation, and prescription cannot be components of revolutionary praxis, precisely because they are components of the praxis of domination. In order to dominate, the dominator has no choice but to deny true praxis to the people, deny them the right to say their own word and think their own thoughts. He and she cannot act dialogically; for to do so would mean either that they had relinquished their power to dominate and joined the cause of the oppressed, or had lost that power through miscalculation.

Obversely, revolutionary leaders who do not act dialogically in their relations with the people either have retained characteristics of the dominator and are not truly revolutionary; or they are totally misguided in their conception of their role, and, prisoners of their own sectarianism, are equally non-revolutionary. They may even reach power. But the validity of any revolution resulting from antidialogical action is thoroughly doubtful.

It is absolutely essential that the oppressed participate in the revolutionary process with an increasingly critical awareness of their role as Subjects of the transformation. If they are drawn into the process as ambiguous beings, partly themselves and partly the oppressors housed within them—and if they come to power still embodying that ambiguity imposed on them by the situation of oppression—it is my contention that they will merely *imagine* they have reached power.[2] Their existential duality may even facilitate the rise of a sectarian climate leading to the installation of bureaucracies which undermine the revolution. If the oppressed do not become aware of this ambiguity during the course of the revolutionary process, they may participate in that process with a spirit more revanchist than revolutionary.[3] They may aspire to revolution as a means of domination, rather than as a road to liberation.

If revolutionary leaders who incarnate a genuine humanism have difficulties and problems, the difficulties and problems will be far greater for a group of leaders who try (even with the best of intentions) to carry out the revolution *for* the people. To attempt this is equivalent to carrying out a revolution *without* the people, because

---

[2] This danger further requires the revolutionary leaders to resist imitating the procedures of the oppressors, who "enter" the oppressed and are "housed" by the latter. The revolutionaries, in their praxis with the oppressed, cannot try to "reside" in the latter. On the contrary, when they try (with the oppressed) to "throw out" the oppressors, they do this in order to live *with* the oppressed—not to live within them.

[3] Although the oppressed, who have always been subject to a regime of exploitation, may understandably impart a revanchist dimension to the revolutionary struggle, the revolution must not exhaust its forces in this dimension.

the people are drawn into the process by the same methods and procedures used to oppress them.

Dialogue with the people is radically necessary to every authentic revolution. This is what makes it a revolution, as distinguished from a military *coup.* One does not expect dialogue from a *coup*—only deceit (in order to achieve "legitimacy") or force (in order to repress). Sooner or later, a true revolution must initiate a courageous dialogue with the people. Its very legitimacy lies in that dialogue.[4] It cannot fear the people, their expression, their effective participation in power. It must be accountable to them, must speak frankly to them of its achievements, its mistakes, its miscalculations, and its difficulties.

The earlier dialogue begins, the more truly revolutionary will the movement be. The dialogue which is radically necessary to revolution corresponds to another radical need: that of women and men as beings who cannot be truly human apart from communication, for they are essentially communicative creatures. To impede communication is to reduce men to the status of "things"—and this is a job for oppressors, not for revolutionaries.

Let me emphasize that my defense of the praxis implies no dichotomy by which this praxis could be divided into a prior stage of reflection and a subsequent stage of action. Action and reflection occur simultaneously. A critical analysis of reality may, however, reveal that a particular form of action is impossible or inappropriate *at the present time.* Those who through reflection perceive the infeasibility or inappropriateness of one or another form of action (which should accordingly be postponed or substituted) cannot thereby be accused of inaction. Critical reflection is also action.

I previously stated that in education the attempt of the teacher-student to understand a cognizable object is not exhausted in that object, because this act extends to other students-teachers in such

---

[4] "While we might obtain some benefit from doubt," said Fidel Castro to the Cuban people as he confirmed the death of Guevara, *"lies, fear* of the truth, complicity with false illusions, and complicity with lies have never been weapons of the revolution." Quoted in *Gramma.* October 17, 1967. Emphasis added.

a way that the cognizable object mediates their capacity for understanding. The same is true of revolutionary action. That is, the oppressed and the leaders are equally the Subjects of revolutionary action, and reality serves as the medium for the transforming action of both groups. In this theory of action one cannot speak of *an actor,* nor simply of *actors,* but rather of *actors in intercommunication.*

This affirmation might appear to imply division, dichotomy, rupture of the revolutionary forces; in fact, it signifies exactly the opposite: their communion. Apart from this communion, we do see dichotomy: leaders on one side and people on the other, in a replica of the relations of oppression. Denial of communion in the revolutionary process, avoidance of dialogue with the people under the pretext of organizing them, of strengthening revolutionary power, or of ensuring a united front, is really a fear of freedom. It is fear of or lack of faith in the people. But if the people cannot be trusted, there is no reason for liberation; in this case the revolution is not even carried out *for the people,* but *"by" the people for the leaders:* a complete self-negation.

The revolution is made neither by the leaders for the people, nor by the people for the leaders, but by both acting together in unshakable solidarity. This solidarity is born only when the leaders witness to it by their humble, loving, and courageous encounter with the people. Not all men and women have sufficient courage for this encounter—but when they avoid encounter they become inflexible and treat others as mere objects; instead of nurturing life, they kill life; instead of searching for life, they flee from it. And these are *oppressor* characteristics.

Some may think that to affirm dialogue—the encounter of women and men in the world in order to transform the world—is naïvely and subjectively idealistic.[5] There is nothing, however, more real or concrete than people in the world and with the world, than humans with other humans—and some people against others, as oppressing and oppressed classes.

---

[5] Once more, let me repeat that this dialogical encounter cannot take place between antagonists.

Authentic revolution attempts to transform the reality which begets this dehumanizing state of affairs. Those whose interests are served by that reality cannot carry out this transformation; it must be achieved by the tyrannized, with their leaders. This truth, however, must become radically consequential; that is, the leaders must *incarnate* it, through communion with the people. In this communion both groups grow together, and the leaders, instead of being simply self-appointed, are installed or authenticated in their praxis with the praxis of the people.

Many persons, bound to a mechanistic view of reality, do not perceive that the concrete situation of individuals conditions their consciousness of the world, and that in turn this consciousness conditions their attitudes and their ways of dealing with reality. They think that reality can be transformed mechanistically,[6] without posing the person's false consciousness of reality as a problem or, through revolutionary action, developing a consciousness which is less and less false. There is no historical reality which is not human. There is no history *without* humankind, and no history *for* human beings; there is only history *of* humanity, made by *people* and (as Marx pointed out) in turn making them. It is when the majorities are denied their right to participate in history as Subjects that they become dominated and alienated. Thus, to supersede their condition as objects by the status of Subjects—the objective of any true revolution—requires that the people act, as well as reflect, upon the reality to be transformed.

It would indeed be idealistic to affirm that, by merely reflecting on oppressive reality and discovering their status as objects, persons have thereby already become Subjects. But while this perception in and of itself does not mean that thinkers have become Subjects, it

---

[6] "The epochs during which the dominant classes are stable, epochs in which the workers' movement must defend itself against a powerful adversary which is occasionally threatening and is in every case solidly seated in power, produces naturally a socialist literature which emphasizes the 'material' element of reality, the obstacles to be overcome, and the scant efficacy of human awareness and action." Goldman, *op. cit.,* pp. 80–81.

*does* mean, as one of my co-investigators[7] affirmed, that they are "Subjects *in expectancy*"—an expectancy which leads them to seek to solidify their new status.

On the other hand, it would be a false premise to believe that activism (which is not true action) is the road to revolution. People will be truly critical if they live the plenitude of the praxis, that is, if their action encompasses a critical reflection which increasingly organizes their thinking and thus leads them to move from a purely naïve knowledge of reality to a higher level, one which enables them to perceive the *causes* of reality. If revolutionary leaders deny this right to the people, they impair their own capacity to think—or at least to think correctly. Revolutionary leaders cannot think *without* the people, nor *for* the people, but only *with* the people.

The dominant elites, on the other hand, can—and do—think without the people—although they do not permit themselves the luxury of failing to think *about* the people in order to know them better and thus dominate them more efficiently. Consequently, any apparent dialogue or communication between the elites and the masses is really the depositing of "communiqués," whose contents are intended to exercise a domesticating influence.

Why do the dominant elites not become debilitated when they do not think with the people? Because the latter constitute their antithesis, their very reason for existence. If the elites were to think with the people, the contradiction would be superseded and they could no longer dominate. From the point of view of the dominators in any epoch, correct thinking presupposes the non-thinking of the people.

A Mr. Giddy, later President of the Royal Society, raised objections which could be matched in every country: "However specious in theory the project might be of giving education to the laboring classes of the poor, it would be prejudicial to their morals and happiness; it would teach them to despise their lot in

---

[7] Fernando García, a Honduran, in a course for Latin Americans (Santiago, 1967).

> life instead of making them good servants in agricultural and
> other laborious employments; instead of teaching them subordi-
> nation it would render them fractious and refractory as was evi-
> dent in the manufacturing counties; it would enable them to
> read seditious pamphlets, vicious books and publications against
> Christianity; it would render them insolent to their superiors
> and in a few years the legislature would find it necessary to
> direct the strong arm of power against them.[8]

What Mr. Giddy really wanted (and what the elites of today want,
although they do not denounce popular education so cynically and
openly) was for the people not to think. Since the Mr. Giddys of all
epochs, as an oppressor class, cannot think *with* the people, neither
can they let the people think for themselves.

The same is not true, however, of revolutionary leaders; if they do
not think with the people, they become devitalized. The people are
their constituent matrix, not mere objects thought of. Although
revolutionary leaders may also have to think about the people in
order to understand them better, this thinking differs from that of
the elite; for in thinking about the people in order to liberate (rather
than dominate) them, the leaders give of themselves to the thinking
of the people. One is the thinking of the *master;* the other is the
thinking of the *comrade.*

Domination, by its very nature, requires only a dominant pole
and a dominated pole in antithetical contradiction; revolutionary
liberation, which attempts to resolve this contradiction, implies the
existence not only of these poles but also of a leadership group which
emerges during this attempt. This leadership group either identifies
itself with the oppressed state of the people, or it is not revolutionary. To simply think *about* the people, as the dominators do, without
any self-giving in that thought, to fail to think *with* the people, is a
sure way to cease being *revolutionary* leaders.

In the process of oppression the elites subsist on the "living death"
of the oppressed and find their authentication in the vertical relationship between themselves and the latter; in the revolutionary

---

[8]   Niebuhr, *op. cit.,* pp. 117–118.

process there is only one way for the emerging leaders to achieve authenticity: they must "die," in order to be reborn through and with the oppressed.

We can legitimately say that in the process of oppression someone oppresses someone else; we cannot say that in the process of revolution someone liberates someone else, nor yet that someone liberates himself, but rather that human beings in communion liberate each other. This affirmation is not meant to undervalue the importance of revolutionary leaders but, on the contrary, to emphasize their value. What could be more important than to live and work with the oppressed, with the "rejects of life," with the "wretched of the earth"? In this communion, the revolutionary leaders should find not only their *raison d'être* but a motive for rejoicing. By their very nature, revolutionary leaders can do what the dominant elites—by their very nature—are unable to do in authentic terms.

Every approach to the oppressed by the elites, as a class, is couched in terms of the false generosity described in chapter 1. But the revolutionary leaders cannot be falsely generous, nor can they manipulate. Whereas the oppressor elites flourish by trampling the people underfoot, the revolutionary leaders can flourish only in communion with the people. Thus it is that the activity of the oppressor cannot be humanist, while that of the revolutionary is necessarily so.

The inhumanity of the oppressors and revolutionary humanism both make use of science. But science and technology at the service of the former are used to reduce the oppressed to the status of "things"; at the service of the latter, they are used to promote humanization. The oppressed must become Subjects of the latter process, however, lest they continue to be seen as mere objects of scientific interest.

Scientific revolutionary humanism cannot, in the name of revolution, treat the oppressed as objects to be analyzed and (based on that analysis) presented with prescriptions for behavior. To do this would be to fall into one of the myths of the oppressor ideology: the *absolutizing of ignorance*. This myth implies the existence of someone who decrees the ignorance of someone else. The one who is doing the decreeing defines himself and the class to which he belongs as those who know or were born to know; he thereby defines others as alien entities. The words of his own class come to be the "true" words, which he imposes or attempts to impose on the others: the oppressed, whose words have been stolen from them. Those who steal the words of others develop a deep doubt in the abilities of the others and consider them incompetent. Each time they say their word without hearing the word of those whom they have forbidden to speak, they grow more accustomed to power and acquire a taste for guiding, ordering, and commanding. They can no longer live without having someone to give orders to. Under these circumstances, dialogue is impossible.

Scientific and humanist revolutionary leaders, on the other hand, cannot believe in the myth of the ignorance of the people. They do not have the right to doubt for a single moment that it is only a myth. They cannot believe that they, and only they, know anything—for this means to doubt the people. Although they may legitimately recognize themselves as having, due to their revolutionary consciousness, a level of revolutionary knowledge different from the level of empirical knowledge held by the people, they cannot impose themselves and their knowledge on the people. They cannot sloganize the people, but must enter into dialogue with them, so that the people's empirical knowledge of reality, nourished by the leaders' critical knowledge, gradually becomes transformed into knowledge of the *causes* of reality.

It would be naïve to expect oppressor elites to denounce the myth which absolutizes the ignorance of the people; it would be a contradiction in terms if revolutionary leaders were *not* to do so, and more contradictory still were they to act in accordance with that myth. The task of revolutionary leaders is to pose as problems not only this myth, but all the other myths used by the oppressor elites to oppress. If, instead, revolutionary leaders persist in imitating the oppressors' methods of domination, the people may respond in either of two ways. In certain historical circumstances, they may become domesticated by the new contents which the leaders deposit in them. In other circumstances, they may become frightened by a "word" which threatens the oppressor housed within them.[9] In neither event do they become revolutionary. In the first case, the revolution is an illusion; in the second case, an impossibility.

Some well-intentioned but misguided persons suppose that since the dialogical process is prolonged[10] (which, incidentally, is not true), they ought to carry out the revolution without communication, by means of "communiqués," and that once the revolution is won, they will *then* develop a thoroughgoing educational effort. They further justify this procedure by saying that it is not possible to carry out education—liberating education—before taking power.

It is worth analyzing some fundamental points of the above asser-

---

[9] Sometimes this "word" is not even spoken. The presence of someone (not necessarily belonging to a revolutionary group) who can threaten the oppressor "housed" in the people is sufficient for the latter to assume destructive positions.

A student once told me how, in a certain Latin American peasant community, a fanatical priest had denounced the presence in the community of two "communists" who were "endangering" what he called the "Catholic faith." That very night the peasants, to a man, joined together to burn alive the two simple elementary school teachers who had been educating the local children. Perhaps that priest had seen in the house of the teachers a book with a bearded man on the cover . . .

[10] Once more, I wish to emphasize that there is no dichotomy between dialogue and revolutionary action. There is not one stage for dialogue and another for revolution. On the contrary, dialogue is the essence of revolutionary action. In the theory of this action, the *actors* intersubjectively direct their action upon an *object* (*reality*, which mediates them) with the humanization of men (to be achieved by transforming that reality) as their objective.

In the theory of oppressor action, antidialogical in essence, the above scheme is simplified. The *actors* have as simultaneous *objects* of their action both *reality* and *the oppressed*, and the preservation of oppression (through the preservation of oppressive reality) as their objective.

|  THEORY OF REVOLUTIONARY ACTION |  | THEORY OF OPPRESSIVE ACTION |
|---|---|---|
| Intersubjectivity |  |  |
| *Subjects-Actors* (revolutionary leaders) | *Actors-Subjects* (the oppressed) | *Actors-Subjects* (dominant elites) |

tions. These men and women (or most of them) believe in the necessity for dialogue with the people, but do not believe this dialogue is feasible prior to taking power. When they deny the possibility that the leaders can behave in a critically educational fashion before taking power, they deny the revolution's educational quality as *cultural action* preparing to become *cultural revolution*. On the other hand, they confuse cultural action with the new education to be inaugurated once power is taken.

I have already affirmed that it would indeed be naïve to expect the oppressor elites to carry out a liberating education. But because the revolution undeniably has an educational nature, in the sense that unless it liberates it is not revolution, the taking of power is only one moment—no matter how decisive—in the revolutionary process. As process, the "before" of the revolution is located within the oppressor society and is apparent only to the revolutionary consciousness.

The revolution is born as a social entity within the oppressor society; to the extent that it is cultural action, it cannot fail to correspond to the potentialities of the social entity in which it originated. Every entity develops (or is transformed) within itself, through the interplay of its contradictions. External conditioners, while necessary, are effective only if they coincide with those potentialities.[11] The newness of the revolution is generated within the old, oppressive society; the taking of power constitutes only a decisive moment

| | Interaction | | | |
|---|---|---|---|---|
| *Object* which mediates | Reality to be transformed | *Object* which mediates | *Object*—the reality to be preserved | *Object*—the oppressed (as part of reality) |
| | for | | for | |
| *Objective* | Humanization as a permanent process | *Objective* | *Objective*—the preservation of oppression | |

[11] See Mao Tse Tung, *op. cit.*

of the continuing revolutionary process. In a dynamic, rather than static, view of revolution, there is no absolute "before" or "after," with the taking of power as the dividing line.

Originating in objective conditions, revolution seeks to supersede the situation of oppression by inaugurating a society of women and men in the process of continuing liberation. The educational, dialogical quality of revolution, which makes it a "cultural revolution" as well, must be present in all its stages. This educational quality is one of the most effective instruments for keeping the revolution from becoming institutionalized and stratified in a counter-revolutionary bureaucracy; for counter-revolution is carried out by revolutionaries who become reactionary.

Were it not possible to dialogue with the people before power is taken, because they have no experience with dialogue, neither would it be possible for the people to come to power, for they are equally inexperienced in the use of power. The revolutionary process is dynamic, and it is in this continuing dynamics, in the praxis of the people with the revolutionary leaders, that the people and the leaders will learn both dialogue and the use of power. (This is as obvious as affirming that a person learns to swim in the water, not in a library.)

Dialogue with the people is neither a concession nor a gift, much less a tactic to be used for domination. Dialogue, as the encounter among men to "name" the world, is a fundamental precondition for their true humanization. In the words of Gajo Petrovic:

A free action can only be one by which a man changes his world and himself . . . A positive condition of freedom is the knowledge of the limits of necessity, the awareness of human creative possibilities . . . The struggle for a free society is not a struggle for a free society unless through it an ever greater degree of individual freedom is created.[12]

---

[12] Gajo Petrovic, "Man and Freedom," in *Socialist Humanism,* edited by Erich Fromm (New York, 1965), pp. 274–276. By the same author, see *Marx in the Mid-Twentieth Century* (New York, 1967).

If this view be true, the revolutionary process is eminently educational in character. Thus the road to revolution involves openness to the people, not imperviousness to them; it involves communion with the people, not mistrust. And, as Lenin pointed out, the more a revolution requires theory, the more its leaders must be *with* the people in order to stand against the power of oppression.

Based on these general propositions, let us undertake a more lengthy analysis of the theories of antidialogical and dialogical action.

## Conquest

The first characteristic of antidialogical action is the necessity for conquest. The antidialogical individual, in his relations with others, aims at conquering them—increasingly and by every means, from the toughest to the most refined, from the most repressive to the most solicitous (paternalism).

Every act of conquest implies a conqueror and someone or something which is conquered. The conqueror imposes his objectives on the vanquished, and makes of them his possession. He imposes his own contours on the vanquished, who internalize this shape and become ambiguous beings "housing" another. From the first, the act of conquest, which reduces persons to the status of things, is necrophilic.

Just as antidialogical action is a concomitant of the real, concrete situation of oppression, dialogical action is indispensable to the revolutionary supersedence of that situation. An individual is not antidialogical or dialogical in the abstract, but in the world. He or she is not first antidialogical, then oppressor; but both, simultaneously. Within an objective situation of oppression, antidialogue is necessary to the oppressor as a means of further oppression—not only economic, but cultural: the vanquished are dispossessed of their word, their expressiveness, their culture. Further, once a situation of oppression has been initiated, antidialogue becomes indispensable to its preservation.

Because liberating action is dialogical in nature, dialogue cannot be a *posteriori* to that action, but must be concomitant with it. And since liberation must be a permanent condition, dialogue becomes a *continuing* aspect of liberating action.[13]

The desire for conquest (or rather the necessity of conquest) is at all times present in antidialogical action. To this end the oppressors attempt to destroy in the oppressed their quality as "considerers" of the world. Since the oppressors cannot totally achieve this destruction, they must *mythicize* the world. In order to present for the consideration of the oppressed and subjugated a world of deceit designed to increase their alienation and passivity, the oppressors develop a series of methods precluding any presentation of the world as a problem and showing it rather as a fixed entity, as something given—something to which people, as mere spectators, must adapt.

It is necessary for the oppressors to approach the people in order, via subjugation, to keep them passive. This approximation, however, does not involve *being with* the people, or require true communication. It is accomplished by the oppressors' depositing myths indispensable to the preservation of the status quo: for example, the myth that the oppressive order is a "free society"; the myth that all persons are free to work where they wish, that if they don't like their boss they can leave him and look for another job; the myth that this order respects human rights and is therefore worthy of esteem; the myth that anyone who is industrious can become an entrepreneur—worse yet, the myth that the street vendor is as much an entrepreneur as the owner of a large factory; the myth of the universal right of education, when of all the Brazilian children who enter primary schools only a tiny fraction ever reach the university; the myth of the equality of all individuals, when the question: "Do you know who you're talking to?" is still current among us; the myth of the

---

[13] Once a popular revolution has come to power, the fact that the new power has the ethical duty to repress any attempt to restore the old oppressive power by no means signifies that the revolution is contradicting its dialogical character. Dialogue between the former oppressors and the oppressed as antagonistic classes was not possible before the revolution; it continues to be impossible afterward.

heroism of the oppressor classes as defenders of "Western Christian civilization" against "materialist barbarism"; the myth of the charity and generosity of the elites, when what they really do as a class is to foster selective "good deeds" (subsequently elaborated into the myth of "disinterested aid," which on the international level was severely criticized by Pope John XXIII);[14] the myth that the dominant elites, "recognizing their duties," promote the advancement of the people, so that the people, in a gesture of gratitude, should accept the words of the elites and be conformed to them; the myth that rebellion is a sin against God; the myth of private property as fundamental to personal human development (so long as oppressors are the only true human beings); the myth of the industriousness of the oppressors and the laziness and dishonesty of the oppressed, as well as the myth of the natural inferiority of the latter and the superiority of the former.[15]

All these myths (and others the reader could list), the internalization of which is essential to the subjugation of the oppressed, are presented to them by well-organized propaganda and slogans, via the mass "communications" media—as if such alienation constituted real communication![16]

In sum, there is no oppressive reality which is not at the same time necessarily antidialogical, just as there is no antidialogue in which the oppressors do not untiringly dedicate themselves to the

---

[14] "Moreover, economically developed countries should take particular care lest, in giving aid to poorer countries, they endeavor to turn the prevailing political situation to their own advantage, and seek to dominate them.

Should perchance such attempts be made, this clearly would be but another form of colonialism which, although disguised in name, merely reflects their earlier but outdated dominion, now abandoned by many countries. When international relations are thus obstructed, the orderly progress of all peoples is endangered." Pope John XXIII, "Christianity and Social Progress," from the Encyclical Letter *Mater et Magistra,* articles 171 and 172.

[15] Memmi refers to the image the colonizer constructs of the colonized: "By his accusation the colonizer establishes the colonized as being lazy. He decides that laziness is constitutional in the very nature of the colonized." Memmi, *op. cit.,* p. 81.

[16] It is not the media themselves which I criticize, but the way they are used.

constant conquest of the oppressed. In ancient Rome, the dominant elites spoke of the need to give "bread and circus" to the people in order to "soften them up" and to secure their own tranquility. The dominant elites of today, like those of any epoch, continue (in a version of "original sin") to need to conquer others—with or without bread and circus. The content and methods of conquest vary historically; what does not vary (as long as dominant elites exist) is the necrophilic passion to oppress.

## Divide and Rule

This is another fundamental dimension of the theory of oppressive action which is as old as oppression itself. As the oppressor minority subordinates and dominates the majority, it must divide it and keep it divided in order to remain in power. The minority cannot permit itself the luxury of tolerating the unification of the people, which would undoubtedly signify a serious threat to their own hegemony. Accordingly, the oppressors halt by any method (including violence) any action which in even incipient fashion could awaken the oppressed to the need for unity. Concepts such as unity, organization, and struggle are immediately labeled as dangerous. In fact, of course, these concepts *are* dangerous—to the oppressors—for their realization is necessary to actions of liberation.

It is in the interest of the oppressor to weaken the oppressed still further, to isolate them, to create and deepen rifts among them. This is done by varied means, from the repressive methods of the government bureaucracy to the forms of cultural action with which they manipulate the people by giving them the impression that they are being helped.

One of the characteristics of oppressive cultural action which is almost never perceived by the dedicated but naïve professionals who are involved is the emphasis on a *focalized* view of problems rather than on seeing them as dimensions of a *totality*. In "community development" projects the more a region or area is broken down into "local communities," without the study of these communities both as totalities in themselves and as parts of another totality (the area, region, and so forth)—which in its turn is part of a still larger totality (the nation, as part of the continental totality)—the more alienation is intensified. And the more alienated people are, the easier it is to divide them and keep them divided. These focalized forms of action, by intensifying the focalized way of life of the oppressed (especially in rural areas), hamper the oppressed from perceiving reality critically and keep them isolated from the problems of oppressed women and men in other areas.[17]

The same divisive effect occurs in connection with the so-called "leadership training courses," which are (although carried out without any such intention by many of their organizers) in the last analysis alienating. These courses are based on the naïve assumption that one can promote the community by training its leaders—as if it were the parts that promote the whole and not the whole which, in being promoted, promotes the parts. Those members of the communities who show sufficient leadership capacities to be chosen for these courses necessarily reflect and express the aspirations of the individuals of their community. They are in harmony with the way of living and thinking about reality which characterizes their comrades, even though they reveal special abilities which give them the status of "leaders." As soon as they complete the course and return to the community with resources they did not formerly possess, they either use these resources to control the submerged and dominated consciousness of their comrades, or they become strangers in their own communities and their former leadership position is thus threatened. In order not to lose their leadership status, they will probably

---

[17] This criticism of course does not apply to actions within a dialectical perspective, based on the understanding of the local community both as a totality in itself and as part of a larger totality. It is directed at those who do not realize that the development of the local community cannot occur except in the total context of which it is a part, in interaction with other parts. This requirement implies the consciousness of unity in diversification, of organization which channels forces in dispersion, and a clear awareness of the necessity to transform reality. This (understandably) is what frightens the oppressors.

tend to continue manipulating the community, but in a more efficient manner.

When cultural action, as a totalized and totalizing process, approaches an entire community and not merely its leaders, the opposite process occurs. Either the former leaders grow along with everyone else, or they are replaced by new leaders who emerge as a result of the new social consciousness of the community.

The oppressors do not favor promoting the community as a whole, but rather selected leaders. The latter course, by preserving a state of alienation, hinders the emergence of consciousness and critical intervention in a total reality. And without this critical intervention, it is always difficult to achieve the unity of the oppressed as a class.

Class conflict is another concept which upsets the oppressors, since they do not wish to consider themselves an oppressive class. Unable to deny, try as they may, the existence of social classes, they preach the need for understanding and harmony between those who buy and those who are obliged to sell their labor.[18] However, the unconcealable antagonism which exists between the two classes makes this "harmony" impossible.[19] The elites call for harmony be-

---

[18] Bishop Franic Split refers eloquently to this point: "If the workers do not become in some way the owners of their labor, all structural reforms will be ineffective. [This is true] even if the workers receive a higher salary in an economic system but are not content with these raises. They want to be owners, not sellers, of their labor. . . . At present the workers are increasingly aware that labor represents a part of the human person. A person, however cannot be bought; neither can he sell himself. Any purchase or sale of labor is a type of slavery. The evolution of human society in this respect is clearly progressing within a system said to be less responsive than our own to the question of human dignity, i.e., Marxism." "15 Obispos hablan en prol del Tercer Mundo." *CIDOC Informa* (Mexico, 1967), Doc. 67/35, pp. 1–11.

[19] With respect to social classes and the struggle between them (which Karl Marx is often accused of inventing), see Marx's letter to J. Weydemeyer dated March 1, 1852: ". . . no credit is due to me for discovering the existence of classes in modern society or the struggle between them. Long before me bourgeois historians had described the historical development of this class struggle and bourgeois economists the economic anatomy of the classes. What I did that was new was to prove: (1) that the existence of classes is only bound up with particular historical phases in the development of production; (2) that the class struggle necessarily leads to the dictatorship of the proletariat; (3) that this dictatorship itself only constitutes

tween classes as if classes were fortuitous agglomerations of individuals curiously looking at a shop window on a Sunday afternoon. The only harmony which is viable and demonstrable is that found among the oppressors themselves. Although they may diverge and upon occasion even clash over group interests, they unite immediately at a threat to the class. Similarly, the harmony of the oppressed is only possible when its members are engaged in the struggle for liberation. Only in exceptional cases is it not only possible but necessary for both classes to unite and act in harmony; but when the emergency which united them has passed they will return to the contradiction which defines their existence and which never really disappeared.

All the actions of the dominant class manifest its need to divide in order to facilitate the preservation of the oppressor state. Its interference in the unions, favoring certain "representatives" of the dominated classes (who actually represent the oppressor, not their own comrades); its promotion of individuals who reveal leadership capacity and could signify a threat if they were not "softened up" in this way; its distribution of benefits to some and penalties to others: all these are ways of dividing in order to preserve the system which favors the elite. They are forms of action which exploit, directly or indirectly, one of the weak points of the oppressed: their basic insecurity. The oppressed are insecure in their duality as beings which "house" the oppressor. On the one hand, they resist her or him; on the other hand, at a certain stage in their relationship, they are attracted by him or her. Under these circumstances, the oppressors easily obtain positive results from divisive action.

In addition, the oppressed know from experience the price of not accepting an "invitation" offered with the purpose of preventing their unity as a class: losing their jobs and finding their names on a "black list" signifying closed doors to other jobs is the least that can happen. Their basic insecurity is thus directly linked to the

---

the transition to the abolition of all classes and to classless society . . ." Karl Marx and Frederick Engels, *Selected Works* (New York, 1968), p. 679.

enslavement of their labor (which really implies the enslavement of their person, as Bishop Split emphasized).

People are fulfilled only to the extent that they create their world (which is a human world), and create it with their transforming labor. The fulfillment of humankind as human beings lies, then, in the fulfillment of the world. If for a person to be in the world of work is to be totally dependent, insecure, and permanently threatened— if their work does not belong to them—the person cannot be fulfilled. Work that is not free ceases to be a fulfilling pursuit and becomes an effective means of dehumanization.

Every move by the oppressed towards unity points towards other actions; it means that sooner or later the oppressed will perceive their state of depersonalization and discover that as long as they are divided they will always be easy prey for manipulation and domination. Unity and organization can enable them to change their weakness into a transforming force with which they can re-create the world and make it more human.[20] The more human world to which they justly aspire, however, is the antithesis of the "human world" of the oppressors—a world which is the exclusive possession of the oppressors, who preach an impossible harmony between themselves (who dehumanize) and the oppressed (who are dehumanized). Since oppressors and oppressed are antithetical, what serves the interests of one group disserves the interests of the others.

Dividing in order to preserve the status quo, then, is necessarily a fundamental objective of the theory of antidialogical action. In addition, the dominators try to present themselves as saviors of the women and men they dehumanize and divide. This messianism, however, cannot conceal their true intention: to save themselves.

---

[20] For this reason it is indispensable for the oppressors to keep the peasants isolated from the urban workers, just as it is indispensable to keep both groups isolated from the students. The testimony of rebellion of the latter (although they do not sociologically constitute a class) makes them dangerous in the event they join the people. It is thus necessary to convince the lower classes that students are irresponsible and disorderly, that their testimony is false because as students they should be studying, just as the factory workers and the peasants should be working towards the "nation's progress."

They want to save their riches, their power, their way of life: the things that enable them to subjugate others. Their mistake is that men *cannot* save themselves (no matter how one understands "salvation"), either as individuals or as an oppressor class. Salvation can be achieved only *with* others. To the extent, however, that the elites oppress, they cannot be *with* the oppressed; for being *against* them is the essence of oppression.

A psychoanalysis of oppressive action might reveal the "false generosity" of the oppressor (described in chapter 1) as a dimension of the latter's sense of guilt. With this false generosity, he attempts not only to preserve an unjust and necrophilic order, but to "buy" peace for himself. It happens that peace cannot be bought; peace is experienced in solidary and loving acts, which cannot be incarnated in oppression. Hence, the messianic element of the theory of antidialogical action reinforces the first characteristic of this action: the necessity for conquest.

Since it is necessary to divide the people in order to preserve the status quo and (thereby) the power of the dominators, it is essential for the oppressors to keep the oppressed from perceiving their strategy. So the former must convince the latter that they are being "defended" against the demonic action of "marginals, rowdies, and enemies of God" (for these are the epithets directed at men who lived and are living the brave pursuit of man's humanization). In order to divide and confuse the people, the destroyers call themselves builders, and accuse the true builders of being destructive. History, however, always takes it upon itself to modify these designations. Today, although the official terminology continues to call Tiradentes[21] a conspirator *("Inconfidente")* and the libertarian movement which he led a conspiracy *("Inconfidência")*, the national hero is not the man[22] who called Tiradentes a "bandit," ordered him

---

[21] *Tiradentes* was leader of an abortive revolt for the independence of Brazil from Portugal in 1789 in Ouro Preto, State of Minas Gerais. This movement is historically called the *Inconfidência Mineira.*—Translator's note.

[22] Visconde de Barbacena, royal administrator of the province.—Translator's note.

hanged and quartered, and had pieces of the bloody corpse strewn through the streets of the neighboring villages as an example. It is Tiradentes who is the hero. History tore up the "title" given him by the elites, and recognized his action for what it was. It is the men who in their own time sought unity for liberation who are the heroes—not those who used their power to divide and rule.

## Manipulation

Manipulation is another dimension of the theory of antidialogical action, and, like the strategy of division, is an instrument of conquest: the objective around which all the dimensions of the theory revolve. By means of manipulation, the dominant elites try to conform the masses to their objectives. And the greater the political immaturity of these people (rural or urban) the more easily the latter can be manipulated by those who do not wish to lose their power.

The people are manipulated by the series of myths described earlier in this chapter, and by yet another myth: the model of itself which the bourgeoisie presents to the people as the possibility for their own ascent. In order for these myths to function, however, the people must accept the word of the bourgeoisie.

Within certain historical conditions, manipulation is accomplished by means of pacts between the dominant and the dominated classes—pacts which, if considered superficially, might give the impression of a dialogue between the classes. In reality, however, these pacts are not dialogue, because their true objectives are determined by the unequivocal interest of the dominant elites. In the last analysis, pacts are used by the dominators to achieve their own ends.[23] The support given by the people to the so-called "national bourgeoisie" in defense of so-called "national capitalism" is an example in

---

[23] Pacts are only valid for the masses (and in this case they are no longer pacts) when the objectives of the action in process or to be developed are subject to their decision.

point. Sooner or later, these pacts always increase the subjugation
of the people. They are proposed only when the people begin (even
naively) to emerge from the historical process and by this emergence to threaten the dominant elites. The presence of the people
in the historical process, no longer as mere spectators, but with the
first signs of aggressivity, is sufficiently disquieting to frighten the
dominant elites into doubling the tactics of manipulation.

In this historical phase, manipulation becomes a fundamental instrument for the preservation of domination. Prior to the emergence
of the people there is no manipulation (precisely speaking), but
rather total suppression. When the oppressed are almost completely
submerged in reality, it is unnecessary to manipulate them. In the
antidialogical theory of action, manipulation is the response of the
oppressor to the new concrete conditions of the historical process.
Through manipulation, the dominant elites can lead the people into
an unauthentic type of "organization," and can thus avoid the threatening alternative: the true organization of the emerged and emerging people.[24] The latter have only two possibilities as they enter the
historical process: either they must organize authentically for their
liberation, or they will be manipulated by the elites. Authentic
organization is obviously not going to be stimulated by the dominators; it is the task of the revolutionary leaders.

It happens, however, that large sectors of the oppressed form an
urban proletariat, especially in the more industrialized centers of
the country. Although these sectors are occasionally restive, they
lack revolutionary consciousness and consider themselves privileged. Manipulation, with its series of deceits and promises, usually
finds fertile ground here.

The antidote to manipulation lies in a critically conscious revolu-

---

[24] In the "organization" which results from acts of manipulation, the people—
mere guided objects—are adapted to the objectives of the manipulators. In true
organization, the individuals are active in the organizing process, and the objectives
of the organization are not imposed by others. In the first case, the organization is a
means of "massification," in the second, a means of liberation. [In Brazilian political
terminology, "massification" is the process of reducing the people to a manageable,
unthinking agglomeration.—Translator]

tionary organization, which will pose to the people as problems their position in the historical process, the national reality, and manipulation itself. In the words of Francisco Weffert:

> All the policies of the Left are based on the masses and depend on the consciousness of the latter. If that consciousness is confused, the Left will lose its roots and certain downfall will be imminent, although (as in the Brazilian case) the Left may be deluded into thinking it can achieve the revolution by means of a quick return to power.[25]

In a situation of manipulation, the Left is almost always tempted by a "quick return to power," forgets the necessity of joining with the oppressed to forge an organization, and strays into an impossible "dialogue" with the dominant elites. It ends by being manipulated by these elites, and not infrequently itself falls into an elitist game, which it calls "realism."

Manipulation, like the conquest whose objectives it serves, attempts to anesthetize the people so they will not think. For if the people join to their presence in the historical process critical thinking about that process, the threat of their emergence materializes in revolution. Whether one calls this correct thinking "revolutionary consciousness" or "class consciousness," it is an indispensable precondition of revolution. The dominant elites are so well aware of this fact that they instinctively use all means, including physical violence, to keep the people from thinking. They have a shrewd intuition of the ability of dialogue to develop a capacity for criticism. While some revolutionary leaders consider dialogue with the people a "bourgeois and reactionary" activity, the bourgeoisie regard dialogue between the oppressed and the revolutionary leaders as a very real danger to be avoided.

One of the methods of manipulation is to inoculate individuals with the bourgeois appetite for personal success. This manipulation is sometimes carried out directly by the elites and sometimes indi-

---

[25] Francisco Weffert, "Politica de massas," *Política e Revolução social no Brasil* (Rio de Janeiro, 1967), p. 187.

rectly, through populist leaders. As Weffert points out, these leaders serve as intermediaries between the oligarchical elites and the people. The emergence of populism as a style of political action thus coincides causally with the emergence of the oppressed. The populist leader who rises from this process is an ambiguous being, an "amphibian" who lives in two elements. Shuttling back and forth between the people and the dominant oligarchies, he bears the marks of both groups.

Since the populist leader simply manipulates, instead of fighting for authentic popular organization, this type of leader serves the revolution little if at all. Only by abandoning his ambiguous character and dual action and by opting decisively for the people (thus ceasing to be populist) does he renounce manipulation and dedicate himself to the revolutionary task of organization. At this point he ceases to be an intermediary between the people and the elites, and becomes a contradiction of the latter; thereupon the elites immediately join forces to curb him. Observe the dramatic and finally unequivocal terms in which Getulio Vargas[26] spoke to the workers at a May 1 celebration during his last period as head of state:

> I want to tell you that the gigantic work of renewal which my Administration is beginning to carry out cannot be completed successfully without the support and the daily, steadfast cooperation of the workers.[27]

Vargas then spoke of his first ninety days in office, which he called "an estimate of the difficulties and obstacles which, here and there, are being raised in opposition to the actions of the government." He spoke directly to the people about how deeply he felt "the helplessness, poverty, the high cost of living, low salaries . . . the hope-

---

[26] Getulio Vargas led the revolution which overthrew Brazilian President Washington Luis in 1930. He remained in power as a dictator until 1945. In 1950 he returned to power as elected president. In August 1954, when the opposition was about to overthrow him, he committed suicide.—Translator's note.

[27] Speech given in Vasco da Gama Stadium on May 1, 1950, *O Governo Trabalhista no Brasil* (Rio), pp. 322–324.

lessness of the unfortunate and the demands of the majority who live in hope of better days."

His appeal to the workers then took on more objective tones:

> I have come to say that at this moment the Administration does not yet have the laws or the concrete instruments for immediate action to defend the people's economy. It is thus necessary for the people *to organize*—not only to defend their own interests, but also to give the government the base of support it requires to carry out its objectives . . . I need your *unity*. I need for you, in solidarity, *to organize* yourselves in unions. I need for you to form a *strong and cohesive bloc* to stand beside the government so that it will have all the force it needs to solve your problems. I need your *unity* so you can fight against *saboteurs,* so you do not fall *prey* to the interests of *speculators* and *rapacious scoundrels* in detriment of the interests of the people. . . . The hour has come to appeal to the workers; unite in your unions as free and organized forces . . . at the present time no Administration can *survive or dispose of sufficient force to achieve its social ends if it does not have the support of the laboring organizations.*[28]

In sum, in this speech Vargas appealed vehemently to the people to organize and to unite in defense of their rights; and he told them, as Chief of State, of the obstacles, the hindrances, and the innumerable difficulties involved in governing *with* them. From that moment on his Administration encountered increasing difficulties, until the tragic climax of August 1954. If Vargas had not in his last term shown such open encouragement to the organization of the people, subsequently linked to a series of measures in defense of the national interest, possibly the reactionary elites would not have taken the extreme measures they did.

Any populist leader who moves (even discreetly) towards the people in any way other than as the intermediary of the oligarchies will be curbed by the latter—if they have sufficient force to stop him. But as long as the leader restricts himself to paternalism and social

---

[28] *Ibid.* Emphasis added.

welfare activities, although there may be occasional divergencies between him and groups of oligarchies whose interests have been touched, deep differences are rare. This is because welfare programs as instruments of manipulation ultimately serve the end of conquest. They act as an anesthetic, distracting the oppressed from the true causes of their problems and from the concrete solution of these problems. They splinter the oppressed into groups of individuals hoping to get a few more benefits for themselves. This situation contains, however, a positive element: the individuals who receive some aid always want more; those who do not receive aid, seeing the example of those who do, grow envious and also want assistance. Since the dominant elites cannot "aid" everyone, they end by increasing the restiveness of the oppressed.

The revolutionary leaders should take advantage of the contradictions of manipulation by posing it as a problem to the oppressed, with the objective of organizing them.

## Cultural Invasion

The theory of antidialogical action has one last fundamental characteristic: cultural invasion, which like divisive tactics and manipulation also serves the ends of conquest. In this phenomenon, the invaders penetrate the cultural context of another group, in disrespect of the latter's potentialities; they impose their own view of the world upon those they invade and inhibit the creativity of the invaded by curbing their expression.

Whether urbane or harsh, cultural invasion is thus always an act of violence against the persons of the invaded culture, who lose their originality or face the threat of losing it. In cultural invasion (as in all the modalities of antidialogical action) the invaders are the authors of, and actors in, the process; those they invade are the objects. The invaders mold; those they invade are molded. The invaders choose; those they invade follow that choice—or are expected to follow it. The invaders act; those they invade have only the illusion of acting, through the action of the invaders.

All domination involves invasion—at times physical and overt, at times camouflaged, with the invader assuming the role of a helping friend. In the last analysis, invasion is a form of economic and cultural domination. Invasion may be practiced by a metropolitan society upon a dependent society, or it may be implicit in the domination of one class over another within the same society.

Cultural conquest leads to the cultural inauthenticity of those who are invaded; they begin to respond to the values, the standards, and the goals of the invaders. In their passion to dominate, to mold others to their patterns and their way of life, the invaders desire to know how those they have invaded apprehend reality—but only so they can dominate the latter more effectively.[29] In cultural invasion it is essential that those who are invaded come to see their reality with the outlook of the invaders rather than their own; for the more they mimic the invaders, the more stable the position of the latter becomes.

For cultural invasion to succeed, it is essential that those invaded become convinced of their intrinsic inferiority. Since everything has its opposite, if those who are invaded consider themselves inferior, they must necessarily recognize the superiority of the invaders. The values of the latter thereby become the pattern for the former. The more invasion is accentuated and those invaded are alienated from the spirit of their own culture and from themselves, the more the latter want to be like the invaders: to walk like them, dress like them, talk like them.

The social *I* of the invaded person, like every social *I*, is formed in the socio-cultural relations of the social stucture, and therefore reflects the duality of the invaded culture. This duality (which was described earlier) explains why invaded and dominated individuals,

---

[29] To this end, the invaders are making increasing use of the social sciences and technology, and to some extent the physical sciences as well, to improve and refine their action. It is indispensable for the invaders to know the past and present of those invaded in order to discern the alternatives of the latter's future and thereby attempt to guide the evolution of that future along lines that will favor their own interests.

at a certain moment of their existential experience, almost "adhere" to the oppressor *Thou*. The oppressed *I* must break with this near adhesion to the oppressor *Thou*, drawing away from the latter in order to see him more objectively, at which point she critically recognizes herself to be in contradiction with the oppressor. In so doing, he "considers" as a dehumanizing reality the structure in which he is being oppressed. This qualitative change in the perception of the world can only be achieved in the praxis.

Cultural invasion is on the one hand an *instrument* of domination, and on the other, the *result* of domination. Thus, cultural action of a dominating character (like other forms of antidialogical action), in addition to being deliberate and planned, is in another sense simply a product of oppressive reality.

For example, a rigid and oppressive social structure necessarily influences the institutions of child rearing and education within that structure. These institutions pattern their action after the style of the structure, and transmit the myths of the latter. Homes and schools (from nurseries to universities) exist not in the abstract, but in time and space. Within the structures of domination they function largely as agencies which prepare the invaders of the future.

The parent-child relationship in the home usually reflects the objective cultural conditions of the surrounding social structure. If the conditions which penetrate the home are authoritarian, rigid, and dominating, the home will increase the climate of oppression.[30] As these authoritarian relations between parents and children intensify, children in their infancy increasingly internalize the paternal authority.

---

[30] Young people increasingly view parent and teacher authoritarianism as inimical to their own freedom. For this very reason, they increasingly oppose forms of action which minimize their expressiveness and hinder their self-affirmation. This very positive phenomenon is not accidental. It is actually a symptom of the historical climate which (as mentioned in chapter 1) characterizes our epoch as an anthropological one. For this reason one cannot (unless he has a personal interest in doing so) see the youth rebellion as a mere example of the traditional differences between generations. Something deeper is involved here. Young people in their rebellion are denouncing and condemning the unjust model of a society of domination. This

Presenting (with his customary clarity) the problem of necrophilia and biophilia, Fromm analyzes the objective conditions which generate each condition, whether in the home (parent-child relations in a climate of indifference and oppression or of love and freedom), or in a sociocultural context. If children reared in an atmosphere of lovelessness and oppression, children whose potency has been frustrated, do not manage during their youth to take the path of authentic rebellion, they will either drift into total indifference, alienated from reality by the authorities and the myths the latter have used to "shape" them; or they may engage in forms of destructive action.

The atmosphere of the home is prolonged in the school, where the students soon discover that (as in the home) in order to achieve some satisfaction they must adapt to the precepts which have been set from above. One of these precepts is not to think.

Internalizing paternal authority through the rigid relationship structure emphasized by the school, these young people tend when they become professionals (because of the very fear of freedom instilled by these relationships) to repeat the rigid patterns in which they were miseducated. This phenomenon, in addition to their class position, perhaps explains why so many professionals adhere to anti-dialogical action.[31] Whatever the specialty that brings them into contact with the people, they are almost unshakably convinced that it is their mission to "give" the latter their knowledge and techniques. They see themselves as "promotors" of the people. Their programs of action (which might have been prescribed by any good theorist of oppressive action) include their own objectives, their own convictions, and their own preoccupations. They do not listen to the people, but instead plan to teach them how to "cast off the laziness

---

rebellion with its special dimension, however, is very recent; society continues to be authoritarian in character.

[31] It perhaps also explains the antidialogical behavior of persons who, although convinced of their revolutionary commitment, continue to mistrust the people and fear communion with them. Unconsciously, such persons retain the oppressor within themselves; and because they "house" the master, they fear freedom.

which creates underdevelopment." To these professionals, it seems absurd to consider the necessity of respecting the "view of the world" held by the people. The professionals are the ones with a "world view." They regard as equally absurd the affirmation that one must necessarily consult the people when organizing the program content of educational action. They feel that the ignorance of the people is so complete that they are unfit for anything except to receive the teachings of the professionals.

When, however, at a certain point of their existential experience, those who have been invaded begin in one way or another to reject this invasion (to which they might earlier have adapted), the professionals, in order to justify their failure, say that the members of the invaded group are "inferior" because they are "ingrates," shiftless," "diseased," or of "mixed blood."

Well-intentioned professionals (those who use "invasion" not as deliberate ideology but as the expression of their own upbringing) eventually discover that certain of their educational failures must be ascribed, not to the intrinsic inferiority of the "simple men of the people," but to the violence of their own act of invasion. Those who make this discovery face a difficult alternative: they feel the need to renounce invasion, but patterns of domination are so entrenched within them that this renunciation would become a threat to their own identities. To renounce invasion would mean ending their dual status as dominated and dominators. It would mean abandoning all the myths which nourish invasion, and starting to incarnate dialogical action. For this very reason, it would mean to cease being *over* or *inside* (as foreigners) in order to be *with* (as comrades). And so the fear of freedom takes hold of these men. During this traumatic process, they naturally tend to rationalize their fear with a series of evasions.

The fear of freedom is greater still in professionals who have not yet discovered for themselves the invasive nature of their action, and who are told that their action is dehumanizing. Not infrequently, especially at the point of decoding concrete situations, training course participants ask the coordinator in an irritated manner:

"Where do you think you're steering us, anyway?" The coordinator isn't trying to "steer" them anywhere; it is just that in facing a concrete situation as a problem, the participants begin to realize that if their analysis of the situation goes any deeper they will either have to divest themselves of their myths, or reaffirm them. Divesting themselves of and renouncing their myths represents, at that moment, an act of self-violence. On the other hand, to reaffirm those myths is to reveal themselves. The only way out (which functions as a defense mechanism) is to project onto the coordinator their own usual practices: *steering, conquering, and invading.*[32]

This same retreat occurs, though on a smaller scale, among men of the people who have been ground down by the concrete situation of oppression and domesticated by charity. One of the teachers of "Full Circle,"[33] which carried out a valuable educational program in New York City under the coordination of Robert Fox, relates the following incident. A group in a New York ghetto was presented a coded situation showing a big pile of garbage on a street corner—the very same street where the group was meeting. One of the participants said at once, "I see a street in Africa or Latin America." "And why not in New York?" asked the teacher. "Because we are the United States and that can't happen here." Beyond a doubt this man and some of his comrades who agreed with him were retreating from a reality so offensive to them that even to acknowledge that reality was threatening. For an alienated person, conditioned by a culture of achievement and personal success, to recognize his situation as objectively unfavorable seems to hinder his own possibilities of success.

In the case cited, and in that of the professionals, the determining force of the culture which develops the myths men subsequently internalize is evident. In both cases, the culture of the dominant class hinders the affirmation of men as beings of decision. Neither

---

[32] See my "Extensão ou Comunicação?" in *Introducción a la Acción Cultural* (Santiago, 1969).

[33] Regarding the activities of this institution, see Mary Cole, *Summer in the City* (New York, 1968).

the professionals nor the discussion participants in the New York slums talk and act for themselves as active Subjects of the historical process. None of them are theoreticians or ideologues of domination. On the contrary, they are *effects* which in turn become *causes* of domination. This is one of the most serious problems the revolution must confront when it reaches power. This stage demands maximum political wisdom, decision, and courage from the leaders, who for this very reason must have sufficient judgment not to fall into irrationally sectarian positions.

Professional women and men of any specialty, university graduates or not, are individuals who have been "determined from above"[34] by a culture of domination which has constituted them as dual beings. (If they had come from the lower classes this miseducation would be the same, if not worse.) These professionals, however, are necessary to the reorganization of the new society. And since many among them—even though "afraid of freedom" and reluctant to engage in humanizing action—are in truth more misguided than anything else, they not only could be, but ought to be, reclaimed by the revolution.

This reclamation requires that the revolutionary leaders, progressing from what was previously dialogical cultural action, initiate the "cultural revolution." At this point, revolutionary power moves beyond its role as a necessary obstacle confronting those who wish to negate humanity, and assumes a new and bolder position, with a clear *invitation* to all who wish to participate in the reconstruction of society. In this sense, "cultural revolution" is a necessary continuation of the dialogical cultural action which must be carried out before the revolution reaches power.

"Cultural revolution" takes the total society to be reconstructed, including all human activities, as the object of its remolding action. Society cannot be reconstructed in a mechanistic fashion; the culture which is culturally recreated through revolution is the fundamental instrument for this reconstruction. "Cultural revolution" is the revo-

---

[34] See Louis Althusser, *Pour Marx* (Paris, 1967), in which he dedicates an entire chapter to *"la dialectique de la surdétermination."*

lutionary regime's maximum effort at *conscientização*—it should reach everyone, regardless of their personal path.

Consequently, this effort at *conscientização* cannot rest content with the technical or scientific training of intended specialists. The new society becomes qualitatively distinct from the old[35] in more than a partial way. Revolutionary society cannot attribute to technology the same ends attributed by the previous society; accordingly, the training of people in the two societies must also differ. Technical and scientific training need not be inimical to humanistic education as long as science and technology in the revolutionary society are at the service of permanent liberation, of humanization.

From this point of view, the training of individuals for any occupation (since all occupations occur in time and space) requires the understanding of (a) culture as a superstructure which can maintain "remnants" of the past[36] alive in the substructure undergoing revolutionary transformation and (b) the occupation itself as an instrument for the transformation of culture. As the cultural revolution deepens *conscientização* in the creative praxis of the new society, people will begin to perceive why mythical remnants of the old society survive in the new. And they will then be able to free themselves more rapidly of these specters, which by hindering the edification of a new society have always constituted a serious problem for every revolution. Through these cultural remnants the oppressor society continues to invade—this time invading the revolutionary society itself.

This invasion is especially terrible because it is carried out not by the dominant elite reorganized as such, but by those who have participated in the revolution. As men who "house" the oppressor, they resist as might the latter themselves the further basic steps which the revolution must take. And as dual beings they also accept (still due to the remnants) power which becomes bureaucratized and which violently represses them. In turn, this violently repressive

---

[35] This process, however, does not occur suddenly, as mechanistic thinkers naïvely assume.
[36] Althusser, *op. cit.*

bureaucratic power can be explained by what Althusser calls the "reactivation of old elements"[37] in the new society each time special circumstances permit.

For all the above reasons, I interpret the revolutionary process as dialogical cultural action which is prolonged in "cultural revolution" once power is taken. In both stages a serious and profound effort at *conscientização*—by means of which the people, through a true praxis, leave behind the status of *objects* to assume the status of historical *Subjects*—is necessary.

Finally, cultural revolution develops the practice of permanent dialogue between leaders and people, and consolidates the participation of the people in power. In this way, as both leaders and people continue their critical activity, the revolution will more easily be able to defend itself against bureaucratic tendencies (which lead to new forms of oppression) and against "invasion" (which is always the same). The invader—whether in a bourgeois or in a revolutionary society—may be an agronomist or a sociologist, an economist or a public health engineer, a priest or a pastor, an educator or a social worker—or a revolutionary.

Cultural invasion, which serves the ends of conquest and the preservation of oppression, always involves a parochial view of reality, a static perception of the world, and the imposition of one world view upon another. It implies the "superiority" of the invader and the "inferiority" of those who are invaded, as well as the imposition of values by the former, who possess the latter and are afraid of losing them.

Cultural invasion further signifies that the ultimate seat of decision regarding the action of those who are invaded lies not with them but with the invaders. And when the power of decision is located outside rather than within the one who should decide, the latter has only the illusion of deciding. This is why there can be no socio-economic development in a dual, "reflex," invaded society. For

---

[37] On this matter, Althusser comments *"Cette reactivation serait proprement inconcevable dans une dialectique dépourvue de surdétermination."* Althusser, *op. cit.*, p. 116.

development to occur it is necessary: a) that there be a movement of search and creativity having its seat of decision in the searcher; b) that this movement occur not only in space, but in the existential time of the conscious searcher.

Thus, while all development is transformation, not all transformation is development. The transformation occurring in a seed which under favorable conditions germinates and sprouts, is not development. In the same way, the transformation of an animal is not development. The transformations of seeds and animals are determined by the species to which they belong; and they occur in a time which does not belong to them, for time belongs to humankind.

Women and men, among the uncompleted beings, are the only ones which develop. As historical, autobiographical, "beings for themselves," their transformation (development) occurs in their own existential time, never outside it. Men who are submitted to concrete conditions of oppression in which they become alienated "beings for another" of the false "being for himself" on whom they depend, are not able to develop authentically. Deprived of their own power of decision, which is located in the oppressor, they follow the prescriptions of the latter. The oppressed only begin to develop when, surmounting the contradiction in which they are caught, they become "beings for themselves."

If we consider society as a being, it is obvious that only a society which is a "being for itself" can develop. Societies which are dual, "reflex," invaded, and dependent on the metropolitan society cannot develop because they are alienated; their political, economic, and cultural decision-making power is located outside themselves, in the invader society. In the last analysis, the latter determines the destiny of the former: mere transformation; for it is their transformation— *not* their development—that is to the interest of the metropolitan society.

It is essential not to confuse modernization with development. The former, although it may affect certain groups in the "satellite society," is almost always induced; and it is the metropolitan society which derives the true benefits therefrom. A society which is merely modernized without developing will continue—even if it takes over some minimal delegated powers of decision—to depend on the outside country. This is the fate of any dependent society, as long as it remains dependent.

In order to determine whether or not a society is developing, one must go beyond criteria based on indices of "per capita" income (which, expressed in statistical form, are misleading) as well as those which concentrate on the study of gross income. The basic, elementary criterion is whether or not the society is a "being for itself." If it is not, the other criteria indicate modernization rather than development.

The principal contradiction of dual societies is the relationship of dependency between them and the metropolitan society. Once the contradiction has been superseded, the transformation hitherto effected through "aid," which has primarily benefitted the metropolitan society, becomes true development, which benefits the "being for itself."

For the above reasons, the purely reformist solutions attempted by these societies (even though some of the reforms may frighten and even panic the more reactionary members of the elite groups) do not resolve their external and internal contradictions. Almost always the metropolitan society induces these reformist solutions in response to the demands of the historical process, as a new way of preserving its hegemony. It is as if the metropolitan society were saying: "Let us carry out reforms before the people carry out a revolution." And in order to achieve this goal, the metropolitan society has no options other than conquest, manipulation, economic and cultural (and sometimes military) invasion of the dependent society—an invasion in which the elite leaders of the dominated society to a large extent act as mere brokers for the leaders of the metropolitan society.

To close this tentative analysis of the theory of antidialogical action, I wish to reaffirm that revolutionary leaders must not use the same antidialogical procedures used by the oppressors; on the contrary, revolutionary leaders must follow the path of dialogue and of communication.

Before proceeding to analyze the theory of dialogical action, it is essential to discuss briefly how the revolutionary leadership group is formed, and some of the historical and sociological consequences for the revolutionary process. Usually this leadership group is made up of men and women who in one way or another have belonged to the social strata of the dominators. At a certain point in their existential experience, under certain historical conditions, these leaders renounce the class to which they belong and join the oppressed, in an act of true solidarity (or so one would hope). Whether or not this adherence results from a scientific analysis of reality, it represents (when authentic) an act of love and true commitment.[38] Joining the oppressed requires going to them and communicating with them. The people must find themselves in the emerging leaders, and the latter must find themselves in the people.

The leaders who have emerged necessarily reflect the contradiction of the dominant elites communicated to them by the oppressed, who may not yet, however, clearly perceive their own state of oppression or critically recognize their relationship of antagonism to the oppressors.[39] They may still be in the position previously termed "adhesion" to the oppressor. On the other hand, it is possible that due to certain objective historical conditions they have already reached a relatively clear perception of their state of oppression.

In the first case, the adhesion—or partial adhesion—of the people to the oppressor makes it impossible for them (to repeat Fanon's point) to locate him *outside* themselves. In the second case, they can locate the oppressor and can thus critically recognize their relationship of antagonism to him.

In the first case, the oppressor is "housed" within the people, and their resulting ambiguity makes them fearful of freedom. They resort (stimulated by the oppressor) to magical explanations or a false

---

[38] The thoughts of Guevara on this subject are cited in the preceding chapter. German Guzman says of Camilo Torres: ". . . he gave everything. At all times he maintained a vital posture of commitment to the people—as a priest, as a Christian, and as a revolutionary." Translated from German Guzman, *Camilo—El Cura Guerrillero* (Bogatá, 1967), p. 5.

[39] "Class necessity" is one thing; "class consciousness" is another.

view of God, to whom they fatalistically transfer the responsibility for their oppressed state.[40] It is extremely unlikely that these self-mistrustful, downtrodden, hopeless people will seek their own liberation—an act of rebellion which they may view as a disobedient violation of the will of God, as an unwarranted confrontation with destiny. (Hence, the oft-emphasized necessity of posing as *problems* the myths fed to the people by the oppressors.) In the second case, when the people have reached a relatively clear picture of oppression which leads them to localize the oppressor outside themselves, they take up the struggle to surmount the contradiction in which they are caught. At this moment they overcome the distance between "class necessity" and "class consciousness."

In the first case, the revolutionary leaders unfortunately and involuntarily become the contradiction of the people. In the second case, the emerging leaders receive from the people sympathetic and almost instantaneous support, which tends to increase during the process of revolutionary action. The leaders go to the people in a spontaneously dialogical manner. There is an almost immediate empathy between the people and the revolutionary leaders: their mutual commitment is almost instantly sealed. In fellowship, they consider themselves co-equal contradictions of the dominant elites. From this point on, the established practice of dialogue between people and leaders is nearly unshakable. That dialogue will continue when power is reached; and the people will know that *they* have come to power.

This sharing in no way diminishes the spirit of struggle, courage, capacity for love, or daring required of the revolutionary leaders. Fidel Castro and his comrades (whom many at the time termed "irresponsible adventurers"), an eminently dialogical leadership group, identified with the people who endured the brutal violence

---

[40] A Chilean priest of high intellectual and moral caliber visiting Recife in 1966 told me: "When a Pernambucan colleague and I went to see several families living in shanties [*mocambos*] in indescribable poverty, I asked them how they could bear to live like that, and the answer was always the same: 'What can I do? It is the will of God and I must accept it.'"

of the Batista dictatorship. This adherence was not easy; it required bravery on the part of the leaders to love the people sufficiently to be willing to sacrifice themselves for them. It required courageous witness by the leaders to recommence after each disaster, moved by undying hope in a future victory which (because forged together *with* the people) would belong not to the leaders alone, but to the leaders *and* the people—or to the people, *including* the leaders.

Fidel gradually polarized the adherence of the Cuban people, who due to their historical experience had already begun to break their adhesion to the oppressor. This "drawing away" from the oppressor led the people to objectify him, and to see themselves as his contradiction. So it was that Fidel never entered into contradiction with the people. (The occasional desertions or betrayals registered by Guevara in his *Relato de la Guerra Revolucionaria*—in which he also refers to the many who adhered—were to be expected.)

Thus, due to certain historical conditions, the movement by the revolutionary leaders to the people is either horizontal—so that leaders and people form one body in contradiction to the oppressor—or it is triangular, with the revolutionary leaders occupying the vertex of the triangle in contradiction to the oppressors and to the oppressed as well. As we have seen, the latter situation is forced on the leaders when the people have not yet achieved a critical perception of oppressive reality.

Almost never, however, does a revolutionary leadership group perceive that it constitutes a contradiction to the people. Indeed, this perception is painful, and the resistance may serve as a defense mechanism. After all, it is not easy for leaders who have emerged through adherence to the oppressed to recognize themselves as being in contradiction with those to whom they adhered. It is important to recognize this reluctance when analyzing certain forms of behavior on the part of revolutionary leaders who involuntarily become a contradiction (although not antagonists) of the people.

In order to carry out the revolution, revolutionary leaders undoubtedly require the adherence of the people. When leaders who constitute a contradiction to the people seek this adherence, and find rather a certain aloofness and mistrust, they often regard this reaction as indicating an inherent defect on the part of the people. They interpret a certain historical moment of the people's consciousness as evidence of their intrinsic deficiency. Since the leaders need the adherence of the people so that the revolution can be achieved (but at the same time mistrust the mistrustful people), they are tempted to utilize the same procedures used by the dominant elites to oppress. Rationalizing their lack of confidence in the people, the leaders say that it is impossible to dialogue with the people before taking power, thus opting for the antidialogical theory of action. Thenceforward—just like the dominant elites—they try to conquer the people: they become messianic; they use manipulation and carry out cultural invasion. By advancing along these paths, the paths of oppression, they will not achieve revolution; or if they do, it will not be authentic revolution.

The role of revolutionary leadership (under any circumstances, but especially so in those described) is to consider seriously, even as they act, the reasons for any attitude of mistrust on the part of the people, and to seek out true avenues of communion with them, ways of helping the people to help themselves critically perceive the reality which oppresses them.

The dominated consciousness is dual, ambiguous, full of fear and mistrust.[41] In his diary about the struggle in Bolivia, Guevara refers several times to the lack of peasant participation:

> The peasant mobilization does not exist, except for informative duties which annoy us somewhat. They are neither very rapid nor very efficient; they can be neutralized. . . . Complete lack of incorporation of the peasants, although they are losing their fear of us and we are succeeding in winning their admiration. It is a slow and patient task.[42]

---

[41] On this point, see Erich Fromm, "The Application of Humanist Psychoanalysis to Marxist Theory," in *Socialist Humanism* (New York, 1966); and Reuben Osborn, *Marxism and Psychoanalysis* (London, 1965).

[42] Che Guevara, *The Secret Papers of a Revolutionary: The Diary of Che Guevara* (The Ramparts Edition, 1968), pp. 105–106, 120.

The internalization of the oppressor by the dominated consciousness of the peasants explains their fear and their inefficiency.

The behavior and reactions of the oppressed, which lead the oppressor to practice cultural invasion, should evoke from the revolutionary a different theory of action. What distinguishes revolutionary leaders from the dominant elite is not only their objectives, but their procedures. If they act in the same way, the objectives become identical. It is as self-contradictory for the dominant elites to pose human-world relations as problems to the people as it is for the revolutionary leaders *not* to do so.

Let us now analyze the theory of dialogical cultural action and attempt to apprehend its constituent elements.

## Cooperation

In the theory of antidialogical action, conquest (as its primary characteristic) involves a Subject who conquers another person and transforms her or him into a "thing." In the dialogical theory of action, Subjects meet in cooperation in order to transform the world. The antidialogical, dominating *I* transforms the dominated, conquered *thou* into a mere *it*.[43] The dialogical *I*, however, knows that it is precisely the *thou* ("not-*I*") which has called forth his or her own existence. He also knows that the *thou* which calls forth his own existence in turn constitutes an *I* which has in his *I* its *thou*. The *I* and the *thou* thus become, in the dialectic of these relationships, two *thous* which become two *I's*.

The dialogical theory of action does not involve a Subject, who dominates by virtue of conquest, and a dominated object. Instead, there are Subjects who meet to *name* the world in order to transform it. If at a certain historical moment the oppressed, for the reasons previously described, are unable to fulfill their vocation as Subjects, the posing of their very oppression as a problem (which always involves some form of action) will help them achieve this vocation.

---

[43] See Martin Buber, *I and Thou* (New York, 1958).

The above does not mean that in the dialogical task there is no role for revolutionary leadership. It means merely that the leaders—in spite of their important, fundamental, and indispensable role—do not own the people and have no right to steer the people blindly towards their salvation. Such a salvation would be a mere gift from the leaders to the people—a breaking of the dialogical bond between them, and a reducing of the people from co-authors of liberating action into the objects of this action.

Cooperation, as a characteristic of dialogical action—which occurs only among Subjects (who may, however, have diverse levels of functions and thus of responsibility)—can only be achieved through communication. Dialogue, as essential communication, must underlie any cooperation. In the theory of dialogical action, there is no place for conquering the people on behalf of the revolutionary cause, but only for gaining their adherence. Dialogue does not impose, does not manipulate, does not domesticate, does not "sloganize." This does not mean, however, that the theory of dialogical action leads nowhere; nor does it mean that the dialogical human does not have a clear idea of what she wants, or of the objectives to which she is committed.

The commitment of the revolutionary leaders to the oppressed is at the same time a commitment to freedom. And because of that commitment, the leaders cannot attempt to conquer the oppressed, but must achieve their adherence to liberation. Conquered adherence is not adherence; it is "adhesion" of the vanquished to the conqueror, who prescribes the options open to the former. Authentic adherence is the free coincidence of choices; it cannot occur apart from communication among people, mediated by reality.

Thus cooperation leads dialogical Subjects to focus their attention on the reality which mediates them and which—posed as a problem —challenges them. The response to that challenge is the action of dialogical Subjects upon reality in order to transform it. Let me re-emphasize that posing reality as a problem does not mean sloganizing: it means critical analysis of a problematic reality.

As opposed to the mythicizing practices of the dominant elites, dialogical theory requires that the world be unveiled. No one can, however, unveil the world *for* another. Although one Subject may initiate the unveiling on behalf of others, the others must also become Subjects of this act. The adherence of the people is made possible by this unveiling of the world and of themselves, in authentic praxis.

This adherence coincides with the trust the people begin to place in themselves and in the revolutionary leaders, as the former perceive the dedication and authenticity of the latter. The trust of the people in the leaders reflects the confidence of the leaders in the people.

This confidence should not, however, be naïve. The leaders must believe in the potentialities of the people, whom they cannot treat as mere objects of their own action; they must believe that the people are capable of participating in the pursuit of liberation. But they must always mistrust the *ambiguity* of oppressed people, mistrust the oppressor "housed" in the latter. Accordingly, when Guevara exhorts the revolutionary to be always mistrustful,[44] he is not disregarding the fundamental condition of the theory of dialogical action. He is merely being a realist.

Although trust is basic to dialogue, it is not an *a priori* condition of the latter; it results from the encounter in which persons are co-Subjects in denouncing the world, as part of the world's transformation. But as long as the oppressor "within" the oppressed is stronger than they themselves are, their natural fear of freedom may lead them to denounce the revolutionary leaders instead! The leaders cannot be credulous, but must be alert for these possibilities. Guevara's *Episodes* confirms these risks: not only desertions, but even betrayal of the cause. At times in this document, while recognizing the necessity of punishing the deserter in order to preserve the

---

[44] Guevara to *El Patojo*, a young Guatemalan leaving Cuba to engage in guerrilla activity in his own country: "Mistrust: at the beginning, do not trust your own shadow, never trust friendly peasants, informers, guides, or contact men. Do not trust anything or anybody until a zone is completely liberated." Che Guevara, *Episodes of the Revolutionary War* (New York, 1968), p. 102.

cohesion and discipline of the group, Guevara also recognizes certain factors which explain the desertion. One of them, perhaps the most important, is the deserter's ambiguity.

Another portion of Guevara's document, which refers to his presence (not only as a guerrilla but as a medical doctor) in a peasant community in the Sierra Maestra and relates to our discussion of cooperation, is quite striking:

> As a result of daily contact with these people and their problems we became *firmly convinced* of the need for a complete change in the life of our people. The idea of an agrarian reform became crystal-clear. *Communion with the people* ceased to be a mere theory, to become an integral part of ourselves.
>
> Guerrillas and peasants began *to merge into a solid mass.* No one can say exactly when, in this long process, the ideas became reality and we *became a part* of the peasantry. As far as I am concerned, the contact with my patients in the Sierra turned a *spontaneous and somewhat lyrical decision* into a *more serene force, one of an entirely different value.* Those poor, suffering, loyal inhabitants of the Sierra cannot even imagine what a *great contribution they made to the forging of our revolutionary ideology.*[45]

Note Guevara's emphasis that *communion* with the people was decisive for the transformation of a "spontaneous and somewhat lyrical decision into a more serene force, one of an entirely different value." It was, then, in dialogue with the peasants that Guevaras revolutionary praxis became definitive. What Guevara did not say, perhaps due to humility, is that it was his own humility and capacity to love that made possible his communion with the people. And this indisputably dialogical communion became cooperation. Note that Guevara (who did not climb the Sierra Maestra with Fidel and his comrades as a frustrated youth in search of adventure) recognizes that his "*communion with the people* ceased to be a mere theory, to become an integral part of [himself]." He stresses how from the

---

[45] *Ibid.*, pp. 56–57. Emphasis added.

moment of that *communion* the peasants became "forgers" of his guerrillas' "revolutionary ideology."

Even Guevara's unmistakable style of narrating his and his comrades' experiences, of describing his contacts with the "poor, loyal" peasants in almost evangelical language, reveals this remarkable man's deep capacity for love and communication. Thence emerges the force of his ardent testimony to the work of another loving man: Camilo Torres, "the guerrilla priest."

Without the communion which engenders true cooperation, the Cuban people would have been mere objects of the revolutionary activity of the men of the Sierra Maestra, and as objects, their adherence would have been impossible. At the most, there might have been "adhesion," but that is a component of domination, not revolution.

In dialogical theory, at no stage can revolutionary action forgo *communion* with the people. *Communion* in turn elicits *cooperation*, which brings leaders and people to the *fusion* described by Guevara. This fusion can exist only if revolutionary action is really *human*, empathetic, loving, communicative, and humble, in order to be liberating.

The revolution loves and creates life; and in order to create life it may be obliged to prevent some men from circumscribing life. In addition to the life-death cycle basic to nature, there is almost an unnatural *living death:* life which is denied its fullness.[46]

It should not be necessary here to cite statistics to show how many Brazilians (and Latin Americans in general) are "living corpses," "shadows" of human beings, hopeless men, women, and children victimized by an endless "invisible war"[47] in which their remnants

---

[46] With regard to man's defenses against his own death, following the "death of God," in current thought, see Mikel Dufrenne, *Pour L'Homme* (Paris, 1968).

[47] "Many [peasants] sell themselves or members of their families into slavery to escape [starvation]. One Belo Horizonte newspaper discovered as many as 50,000 victims (sold for $1,500,000), and one reporter, to prove it, bought a man and his wife for $30. 'I have seen many a good man starve,' explained the slave; 'that is why I did not mind being sold.' When one slave dealer was arrested in São Paulo in 1959, he admitted having contacts with São Paulo ranchers, coffee plantations,

of life are devoured by tuberculosis, schistosomiasis, infant diarrhea
. . . by the myriad diseases of poverty (most of which, in the terminology of the oppressors, are called "tropical diseases").

Father Chenu makes the following comments regarding possible
reactions to situations as extreme as the above:

> Many, both among the priests attending the Council and the
> informed laymen, fear that in facing the needs and suffering of
> the world we may simply adopt an emotional protest in favor of
> palliating the manifestations and symptoms of poverty and in-
> justice without going on to analyze the causes of the latter, to
> denounce a regime which encompasses this injustice and engen-
> ders 'his poverty.[48]

## Unity for Liberation

Whereas in the antidialogical theory of action the dominators are
compelled by necessity to divide the oppressed, the more easily to
preserve the state of oppression, in the dialogical theory the leaders
must dedicate themselves to an untiring effort for unity among the
oppressed—and unity of the leaders with the oppressed—in order
to achieve liberation.

The difficulty is that this category of dialogical action (like the
others) cannot occur apart from the praxis. The praxis of oppression
is easy (or at least not difficult) for the dominant elite; but it is not
easy for the revolutionary leaders to carry out a liberating praxis.
The former group can rely on using the instruments of power; the
latter group has this power directed against it. The former group
can organize itself freely, and though it may undergo fortuitous and
momentary divisions, it unites rapidly in the face of any threat to
its fundamental interests. The latter group cannot exist without the

---

and construction projects for his commodity—except teenage girls who were sold
to brothels." John Gerassi, *The Great Fear* (New York, 1963).

[48] M.-D. Chenu, *Temoignage Chrétien*, April 1964, as cited by André Moine,
in *Christianos y Marxistas después del Concilio* (Bueno Aires, 1965), p. 167.

people, and this very condition constitutes the first obstacle to its efforts at organization.

It would indeed be inconsistent of the dominant elite to allow the revolutionary leaders to organize. The internal unity of the dominant elite, which reinforces and organizes its power, requires that the people be divided; the unity of the revolutionary leaders only exists in the unity of the people among themselves and in turn with them. The unity of the elite derives from its *antagonism* with the people; the unity of the revolutionary leadership group grows out of *communion* with the (united) people. The concrete situation of oppression—which dualizes the *I* of the oppressed, thereby making the oppressed person ambiguous, emotionally unstable, and fearful of freedom—facilitates the divisive action of the dominator by hindering the unifying action indispensable to liberation.

Further, domination is itself *objectively* divisive. It maintains the oppressed *I* in a position of "adhesion" to a reality which seems all-powerful and overwhelming, and then alienates by presenting mysterious forces to explain this power. Part of the oppressed *I* is located in the reality to which it "adheres"; part is located outside the self, in the mysterious forces which are regarded as responsible for a reality about which nothing can be done. The individual is divided between an identical past and present, and a future without hope. He or she is a person who does not perceive himself or herself as *becoming;* hence cannot have a future to be built in unity with others. But as he or she breaks this "adhesion" and objectifies the reality from which he or she starts to emerge, the person begins to integrate as a Subject (an *I*) confronting an object (reality). At this moment, sundering the false unity of the divided self, one becomes a true individual.

To divide the oppressed, an ideology of oppression is indispensable. In contrast, achieving their unity requires a form of cultural action through which they come to know the *why* and *how* of their adhesion to reality—it requires de-ideologizing. Hence, the effort to unify the oppressed does not call for mere ideological "sloganizing." The latter, by distorting the authentic relation between the Subject and objective reality, also separates the *cognitive,* the *affective,* and the *active* aspects of the total, indivisible personality.

The object of dialogical-libertarian action is not to "dislodge" the oppressed from a mythological reality in order to "bind" them to another reality. On the contrary, the object of dialogical action is to make it possible for the oppressed, by perceiving their adhesion, to opt to transform an unjust reality.

Since the unity of the oppressed involves solidarity among them, regardless of their exact status, the unity unquestionably requires class consciousness. However, the submersion in reality which characterizes the peasants of Latin America means that consciousness of being an oppressed class must be preceded (or at least accompanied) by achieving consciousness of being oppressed individuals.[49]

Proposing as a problem, to a European peasant, the fact that he or she is a person might strike them as strange. This is not true of Latin-American peasants, whose world usually ends at the boundaries of the latifundium, whose gestures to some extent simulate those of the animals and the trees, and who often consider themselves equal to the latter.

Men who are bound to nature and to the oppressor in this way must come to discern themselves as *persons* prevented from *being*. And discovering themselves means in the first instance discovering themselves as *Pedro*, as *Antonio*, or as *Josefa*. This discovery implies a different perception of the meaning of designations: the words "world," "men," "culture," "tree," "work," "animal," reassume their true significance. The peasants now see themselves as transformers of reality (previously a mysterious entity) through their creative labor. They discover that—as people—they can no longer continue to be "things" possessed by others; and they can move from consciousness of themselves as oppressed individuals to the consciousness of an oppressed class.

Any attempt to unify the peasants based on activist methods

---

[49] For someone to achieve critical consciousness of his status as an oppressed man requires recognition of his reality as an oppressive reality. For this very reason, it requires reaching the *"compréhension de l'essence de la societé,"* which is for Lukács *"un facteur de puissance de tout premier ordre, pouquoi c'est même sans doute l'arme purement et simplement dévisive . . ."* Georg Lukács, *Histoire et Conscience de Classe* (Paris, 1960), p. 93.

which rely on "slogans" and do not deal with these fundamental aspects produces a mere juxtaposition of individuals, giving a purely mechanistic character to their action. The unity of the oppressed occurs at the human level, not at the level of things. It occurs in a reality which is only authentically comprehended in the dialectic between the sub- and superstructure.

In order for the oppressed to unite, they must first cut the umbilical cord of magic and myth which binds them to the world of oppression; the unity which links them to each other must be of a different nature. To achieve this indispensable unity the revolutionary process must be, from the beginning, *cultural action*. The methods used to achieve the unity of the oppressed will depend on the latter's historical and existential experience within the social structure.

Peasants live in a "closed" reality with a single, compact center of oppressive decision; the urban oppressed live in an expanding context in which the oppressive command center is plural and complex. Peasants are under the control of a dominant figure who incarnates the oppressive system; in urban areas, the oppressed are subjected to an "oppressive impersonality." In both cases the oppressive power is to a certain extent "invisible": in the rural zone, because of its proximity to the oppressed; in the cities, because of its dispersion.

Forms of cultural action in such different situations as these have nonetheless the same objective: to clarify to the oppressed the objective situation which binds them to the oppressors, visible or not. Only forms of action which avoid mere speech-making and ineffective "blah" on the one hand, and mechanistic activism on the other, can also oppose the divisive action of the dominant elites and move towards the unity of the oppressed.

## Organization

In the theory of antidialogical action, manipulation is indispensable to conquest and domination; in the dialogical theory of action the organization of the people presents the antagonistic opposite of this manipulation. Organization is not only directly linked to unity, but is a natural development of that unity. Accordingly, the leaders' pursuit of unity is necessarily also an attempt to organize the people, requiring witness to the fact that the struggle for liberation is a common task. This constant, humble, and courageous witness emerging from cooperation in a shared effort—the liberation of women and men—avoids the danger of antidialogical control. The form of witness may vary, depending on the historical conditions of any society; witness itself, however, is an indispensable element of revolutionary action.

In order to determine the *what* and *how* of that witness, it is therefore essential to have an increasingly critical knowledge of the current historical context, the view of the world held by the people, the principal contradiction of society, and the principal aspect of that contradiction. Since these dimensions of witness are historical, dialogical, and therefore dialectical, witness cannot simply import them from other contexts without previously analyzing its own. To do otherwise is to absolutize and mythologize the relative; alienation then becomes unavoidable. Witness, in the dialogical theory of action, is one of the principal expressions of the cultural and educational character of the revolution.

The essential elements of witness which do not vary historically include: *consistency* between words and actions; *boldness* which urges the witnesses to confront existence as a permanent risk; *radicalization* (not sectarianism) leading both the witnesses and the ones receiving that witness to increasing action; *courage to love* (which, far from being accommodation to an unjust world, is rather the transformation of that world in behalf of the increasing liberation of humankind); and *faith* in the people, since it is to them that witness is made—although witness to the people, because of their dialectical relations with the dominant elites, also affects the latter (who respond to that witness in their customary way).

All authentic (that is, critical) witness involves the daring to run risks, including the possibility that the leaders will not always win the immediate adherence of the people. Witness which has not borne fruit at a certain moment and under certain conditions is not thereby rendered incapable of bearing fruit tomorrow. Since witness is not an abstract gesture, but an action—a confrontation with the world and with people—it is not static. It is a dynamic element which becomes part of the societal context in which it occurred; from that moment, it does not cease to affect that context.[50]

In antidialogical action, manipulation anesthetizes the people and facilitates their domination; in dialogical action manipulation is superseded by authentic organization. In antidialogical action, manipulation serves the ends of conquest; in dialogical action, daring and loving witness serve the ends of organization.

For the dominant elites, organization means organizing themselves. For the revolutionary leaders, organization means organizing themselves *with* the people. In the first event, the dominant elite increasingly structures its power so that it can more efficiently dominate and depersonalize; in the second, organization only corresponds to its nature and objective if in itself it constitutes the practice of freedom. Accordingly, the discipline necessary to any organization must not be confused with regimentation. It is quite true that without leadership, discipline, determination, and objectives—without tasks to fulfill and accounts to be rendered—an organization cannot survive, and revolutionary action is thereby diluted. This fact, however, can never justify treating the people as things to be used. The people are already depersonalized by oppression—if the revolutionary leaders manipulate them, instead of working towards their *conscientização,* the very objective of organization (that is, liberation) is thereby negated.

Organizing the people is the process in which the revolutionary leaders, who are also prevented from saying their own word,[51] initi-

---

[50] Regarded as process, authentic witness which does not bear immediate fruit cannot be judged an absolute failure. The men who butchered Tiradentes could quarter his body, but they could not erase his witness.

[51] Dr. Orlando Aguirre Ortiz, Director of a Medical School at a Cuban university, once told me: "The revolution involves three "P's": *palavra, povo, e pólvora* [word, people, and gunpowder]. The explosion of the gunpowder clears the people's perception of their concrete situation, in pursuit, through action, of their libera-

ate the experience of learning how to *name* the world. This is true learning experience, and therefore dialogical. So it is that the leaders cannot say their word alone; they must say it *with* the people. Leaders who do not act dialogically, but insist on imposing their decisions, do not organize the people—they manipulate them. They do not liberate, nor are they liberated: they oppress.

The fact that the leaders who organize the people do not have the right to arbitrarily impose their word does not mean that they must therefore take a liberalist position which would encourage license among the people, who are accustomed to oppression. The dialogical theory of action opposes both authoritarianism and license, and thereby affirms authority and freedom. There is no freedom without authority, but there is also no authority without freedom. All freedom contains the possibility that under special circumstances (and at different existential levels) it may become authority. Freedom and authority cannot be isolated, but must be considered in relationship to each other.[52]

Authentic authority is not affirmed as such by a mere *transfer* of power, but through *delegation* or in sympathetic *adherence*. If authority is merely transferred from one group to another, or is imposed upon the majority, it degenerates into authoritarianism. Authority can avoid conflict with freedom only if it is "freedom-become-authority." Hypertrophy of the one provokes atrophy of the other. Just as authority cannot exist without freedom, and vice versa, authoritarianism cannot exist without denying freedom, nor license without denying authority.

In the theory of dialogical action, organization requires authority, so it cannot be authoritarian; it requires freedom, so it cannot be licentious. Organization is, rather, a highly educational process in which leaders and people together experience true authority and

---

tion." It was interesting to observe how this revolutionary physician stressed the *word* in the sense it has been used in this essay: as action and reflection, as praxis.

[52] This relationship will be conflictive if the objective situation is one of oppression or of license.

freedom, which they then seek to establish in society by trans-forming the reality which mediates them.

## Cultural Synthesis

Cultural action is always a systematic and deliberate form of action which operates upon the social structure, either with the objective of preserving that structure or of transforming it. As a form of delib-erate and systematic action, all cultural action has its theory which determines its ends and thereby defines its methods. Cultural action either serves domination (consciously or unconsciously) or it serves the liberation of men and women. As these dialectically opposed types of cultural action operate in and upon the social structure, they create dialectical relations of *permanence* and *change.*

The social structure, in order to *be,* must *become;* in other words, *becoming* is the way the social structure expresses *"duration,"* in the Bergsonian sense of the term.[53]

Dialogical cultural action does not have as its aim the disappear-ance of the permanence-change dialectic (an impossible aim, since disappearance of the dialectic would require the disappearance of the social structure itself and thus of men); it aims, rather, at sur-mounting the antagonistic contradictions of the social structure, thereby achieving the liberation of human beings.

Antidialogical cultural action, on the other hand, aims at mythiciz-ing such contradictions, thereby hoping to avoid (or hinder insofar as possible) the radical transformation of reality. Antidialogical action explicitly or implicitly aims to preserve, within the social structure, situations which favor its own agents. While the latter would never accept a transformation of the structure sufficiently radical to over-come its antagonistic contradictions, they may accept reforms which

---

[53] What makes a structure a *social* structure (and thus historical-cultural) is neither permanence nor change, taken absolutely, but the dialectical relations be-tween the two. In the last analysis, what endures in the social structure is neither permanence nor change; it is the permanence-change dialectic itself.

do not affect their power of decision over the oppressed. Hence, this modality of action involves the *conquest* of the people, their *division,* their *manipulation,* and *cultural invasion.* It is necessarily and fundamentally an *induced* action. Dialogical action, however, is characterized by the supersedence of any induced aspect. The incapacity of antidialogical cultural action to supersede its induced character results from its objective: domination; the capacity of dialogical cultural action to do this lies in its objective: liberation.

In cultural invasion, the actors draw the thematic content of their action from their own values and ideology; their starting point is their own world, from which they enter the world of those they invade. In cultural synthesis, the actors who come from "another world" to the world of the people do so not as invaders. They do not come to *teach* or to *transmit* or to *give* anything, but rather to learn, with the people, about the people's world.

In cultural invasion the actors (who need not even go personally to the invaded culture; increasingly, their action is carried out by technological instruments) superimpose themselves on the people, who are assigned the role of spectators, of objects. In cultural synthesis, the actors become integrated with the people, who are co-authors of the action that both perform upon the world.

In cultural invasion, both the spectators and the reality to be preserved are objects of the actors' action. In cultural synthesis, there are no spectators; the object of the actors' action is the reality to be transformed for the liberation of men.

Cultural synthesis is thus a mode of action for confronting culture itself, as the preserver of the very structures by which it was formed. Cultural action, as historical action, is an instrument for superseding the dominant alienated and alienating culture. In this sense, every authentic revolution is a cultural revolution.

The investigation of the people's generative themes or meaningful thematics described in chapter 3 constitutes the starting point for the process of action as cultural synthesis. Indeed, it is not really possible to divide this process into two separate steps; first, *thematic investigation,* and then *action as cultural synthesis.* Such a dichotomy would imply an initial phase in which the people, as passive objects, would be studied, analyzed, and investigated by the investigators—a procedure congruent with antidialogical action. Such division would lead to the naïve conclusion that action as synthesis follows from action as invasion.

In dialogical theory, this division cannot occur. The Subjects of thematic investigation are not only the professional investigators but also the men and women of the people whose thematic universe is being sought. Investigation—the first moment of action as cultural synthesis—establishes a climate of creativity which will tend to develop in the subsequent stages of action. Such a climate does not exist in cultural invasion, which through alienation kills the creative enthusiasm of those who are invaded, leaving them hopeless and fearful of risking experimentation, without which there is no true creativity.

Those who are invaded, whatever their level, rarely go beyond the models which the invaders prescribe for them. In cultural synthesis there are no invaders; hence, there are no imposed models. In their stead, there are actors who critically analyze reality (never separating this analysis from action) and intervene as Subjects in the historical process.

Instead of following predetermined plans, leaders and people, mutually identified, together create the guidelines of their action. In this synthesis, leaders and people are somehow reborn in new knowledge and new action. Knowledge of the alienated culture leads to transforming action resulting in a culture which is being freed from alienation. The more sophisticated knowledge of the leaders is remade in the empirical knowledge of the people, while the latter is refined by the former.

In cultural synthesis—and only in cultural synthesis—it is possible to resolve the contradiction between the world view of the leaders and that of the people, to the enrichment of both. Cultural synthesis does not deny the differences between the two views; indeed, it is based on these differences. It *does* deny the *invasion* of one *by* the other, but affirms the undeniable *support* each gives *to* the other.

Revolutionary leaders must avoid organizing themselves apart from the people; whatever contradiction to the people may occur fortuitously, due to certain historical conditions, must be solved—not augmented by the cultural invasion of an imposed relationship. Cultural synthesis is the only way.

Revolutionary leaders commit many errors and miscalculations by not taking into account something so real as the people's view of the world: a view which explicitly and implicitly contains their concerns, their doubts, their hopes, their way of seeing the leaders, their perceptions of themselves and of the oppressors, their religious beliefs (almost always syncretic), their fatalism, their rebellious reactions. None of these elements can be seen separately, for in interaction all of them compose a totality. The oppressor is interested in knowing this totality only as an aid to his action of invasion in order to dominate or preserve domination. For the revolutionary leaders, the knowledge of this totality is indispensable to their action as cultural synthesis.

Cultural synthesis (precisely because it is a *synthesis*) does not mean that the objectives of revolutionary action should be limited by the aspirations expressed in the world view of the people. If this were to happen (in the guise of respect for that view), the revolutionary leaders would be passively bound to that vision. Neither invasion by the leaders of the people's world view nor mere adaptation by the leaders to the (often naive) aspirations of the people is acceptable.

To be concrete: if at a given historical moment the basic aspiration of the people goes no further than a demand for salary increases, the leaders can commit one of two errors. They can limit their action to stimulating this one demand[54] or they can overrule this popular aspiration and substitute something more far-reaching—but something which has not yet come to the forefront of the people's attention. In the first case, the revolutionary leaders follow a line of

---

[54] Lenin severely attacked the tendency of the Russian Social Democratic Party to emphasize economic demands of the proletariat as an instrument of the revolutionary struggle, a practice he termed "economic spontaneity." "What is to be Done?" in *On Politics and Revolution, Selected Writings* (New York, 1968).

adaptation to the people's demands. In the second case, by disrespecting the aspirations of the people, they fall into cultural invasion.

The solution lies in synthesis: the leaders must on the one hand identify with the people's demand for higher salaries, while on the other they must pose the meaning of that very demand as a problem. By doing this, the leaders pose as a problem a real, concrete, historical situation of which the salary demand is one dimension. It will thereby become clear that salary demands alone cannot comprise a definitive solution. The essence of this solution can be found in the previously cited statement by bishops of the Third World that "if the workers do not somehow come to be owners of their own labor, all structural reforms will be ineffective . . . they [must] be owners, not sellers, of their labor . . . [for] any purchase or sale of labor is a type of slavery."

To achieve critical consciousness of the facts that it is necessary to be the "owner of one's own labor," that labor "constitutes part of the human person," and that "a human being can neither be sold nor can he sell himself" is to go a step beyond the deception of palliative solutions. It is to engage in authentic transformation of reality in order, by humanizing that reality, to humanize women and men.

In the antidialogical theory of action, cultural invasion serves the ends of manipulation, which in turn serves the ends of conquest, and conquest the ends of domination. Cultural synthesis serves the ends of organization; organization serves the ends of liberation.

This work deals with a very obvious truth: just as the oppressor, in order to oppress, needs a theory of oppressive action, so the oppressed, in order to become free, also need a theory of action.

The oppressor elaborates his theory of action without the people, for he stands against them. Nor can the people—as long as they are crushed and oppressed, internalizing the image of the oppressor—construct by themselves the theory of their liberating action. Only in the encounter of the people with the revolutionary leaders—in their communion, in their praxis—can this theory be built.

# *"A luta continua"*: Afterword to *Pedagogy of the Oppressed*

Ira Shor, College of Staten Island, CUNY, USA

> *Now I am no longer part of the "masses," I am "people" and I can demand my rights.*
>
> Francisca Andrade, student in a Freirean literacy circle in Angicos, 1963
> (Kirkendall, 40)

The Angicos literacy circle celebrated its final meeting April 2, 1963, with not only Paulo Freire in attendance but also the liberal President of the Republic, Joao Goulart. Freire told the President, there "exists today a people who decides, a people that is rising up, a people that has begun to become aware of its destiny and has begun to take part in the Brazilian historical process irreversibly."(Kirkendall, 40) At that ceremony, another dignitary attending was General Humberto Castelo Branco who, one year later almost to the day, would reverse democracy by overthrowing Goulart, crushing Paulo's national program, and throwing Paulo in jail.

The lights went out in Brazil for too many years after that. Perhaps I can say that this book was born in the dark, or better, born *against* the dark, or better yet, born for hope and resistance against oppression. Part of an advancing democratic movement in Brazil, Freire's method taught illiterates to read and write in only 40 hours of inexpensive instruction. Once basically literate, poor peasants and workers could finally qualify to vote after a very long silence imposed from the top down, vastly expanding the electorate from the bottom up. If thousands of Freirean culture circles had opened as planned after that terrible April 1964, millions of working-class illiterates would read and write well enough to register as new voters, pulling political power to the majority. To stop such a democratic possibility, the oligarchy and its army overthrew the elected Goulart administration which had appointed Freire to his national post. Interrogated and jailed, Freire was forced to leave the country. He then wandered the world with his wife Elza and five children until 1980, his books banned in Brazil, evicted from his homeland in the prime of his political life. Others who could not escape were imprisoned, beaten, or hounded as the generals restored a conservative elite to unaccountable power. In the years ahead, Paulo would use his survival well, addressing large crowds in Europe and North America as well as consulting with governments, NGOs, and local projects, becoming the most famous educator of his time as well as a foremost advocate for social justice, producing *A Pedagogy of the Oppressed* while the wounds of the coup were still fresh: "Problem-posing education is revolutionary futurity…Any situation in which some individuals prevent others from engaging in the process of inquiry is one of violence."(*65, 66*)

Few books have been so widely debated, quoted, excerpted, and also used for teacher education, graduate and undergraduate courses, and in some high schools (as the banning of this book in Tucson in 2012 showed). Fifty years later, what can explain the extraordinary appeal of *Pedagogy of the Oppressed*?

In four brief chapters, Paulo Freire integrated a remarkable array of concerns:

1. A theory and a practice for a critical pedagogy to question the status quo in the name of social justice.
2. The theory and practice involved a "situated pedagogy" which could be adapted for diverse places, different stakeholders, and varying conditions.
3. This situated pedagogy provided a rich lexicon of practice: a dialogue method of instruction, "problem-posing inquiry" instead of "banking pedagogy" memorization, "untested feasibility," "limit-situations and limit-acts," "the culture circle," "the teacher-student with students-teachers," "the vocabulary universe," "the generative theme and the generative word,"

"codification and de-codification," *conscientization* or coming to critical consciousness, "hinged themes" and "the anthropological notion of culture," *praxis* or action/reflection—cyclically theorizing practice and practicing theory.

4. This lexicon for critical theory and practice evolved as Paulo experimented before the coup for fifteen years in adult literacy education outside formal school systems; later, it would be adapted for k-12 and higher education units.

5. Open to diverse settings for critical practice, this book crossed paths with multicultural, anti-racist and feminist pedagogies and movements also emerging at that time with similar orientations toward equality, democracy, and social justice.

6. The social justice orientation of this book appeared just when mass movements for radical change became global phenomena, in a period famous for "the immense and proliferating criticizability of things, institutions and practices, and discourses," as Michel Foucault put it,(6) and when student-centered approaches and constructivist methods were on the offensive in educational circles.

7. Student-centered, constructivist, and critical of inequality, Freire's theory and practice proposed all education as politics. No pedagogy can be neutral because all develop human subjects and produce consciousness one way or another, depending on the ideology of the contents, the social relations of discourse, and the learning process of the curriculum. Any pedagogy or curriculum which does not question the status quo tacitly or actively endorses it.

8. This learning process offered appealing moral values based in ethics of mutuality and professional responsibility to teach for a world less violent and cruel. Freire's preoccupation with humanization and de-humanization launched this concern on the very first page.

9. Finally, "Chapter 4" is an extraordinary epistle to would-be revolutionary leaders, not merely advice for critical educators. It rebukes oppositional leaders who denounce domination but slide into authoritarian monologue, exhortation, abstractness, bureaucratic rule, and propagandizing (not permissible in Freirean classrooms).

These points help account for the longevity and impact of this small book, which was not written as a scholastic treatise, but rather grew from Freire's reflection on his practice and experiences. "Thought and study alone did not produce *Pedagogy of the Oppressed*," Freire wrote in "The Preface." This book, he reported, "is rooted in concrete situations and describes the reactions of laborers (peasant or urban) and of middle-class persons whom I have observed directly or indirectly during the course of my educative work."(19)

Paulo considered critical education in schools or in social movements intellectually demanding and politically risky. Movements with internal education programs confront formidable authorities who Paulo called "the power now in power." In schools and colleges, teachers and students make themselves each day but under terms largely dominated from outside and above ("limit-situations" against which critical pedagogy is a "limit-act"). Paulo was especially oriented to the critical learning possible inside mass movements("the power not yet in power"), but found himself appointed Secretary of Education for Sao Paulo's 643 schools when the Workers Party won control of that city administration in 1989. For Paulo, throughout his life and work, the essential questions of this famous book remained: What kind of world do we live in? Why is it like that? What kind of world do we want? How do we get there from here?

April 2017, New York, USA

## References

Foucault, Michel, *"Society Must Be Defended"*. Picador: New York. Translated by David Macey, 2003.

Freire, Paulo, *Pedagogy of the Oppressed*. Continuum: New York. Translated by Myra Bergman Ramos. Rev. 20th Anniversary Edition, 1993.

Kirkendall, Andrew J., *Paulo Freire and the Cold War Politics of Literacy*. UNC Press: Chapel Hill, 2010.

# Interviews with
# Contemporary Scholars

# Marina Aparicio Barberán

*Paulo Freire Institute, Spain*

**Please tell us about your background and current areas of expertise.**

I am a political scientist (with an undergraduate degree from Pompeu Fabra University), and I specialize in public and social policy analysis and evaluation (with two master's degrees from UPF-John Hopkins and Valencia-UVEG). My research areas are policy analysis, political and electoral behavior, and political and parliamentary elites analysis.

**How did you come to read Freire's *Pedagogy of the Oppressed* for the first time?**

My first time reading *Pedagogy of the Oppressed* was in 2006; I was a participant and collaborative member of the Centro de Recursos y Educación Contínua (CREC-Diputación de Valencia) directed by Pep Aparicio Guadas (1999/2013). In this center I conducted publishing tasks and took on organizational and educational functions related to my training and field. At the same time, I continued with my studies in political science, as well as various activities within social movements.

Previously, I had read some of Freire's other works, but I think it is important to note how this book enticed me . . . the analysis, the words and the way Freire articulates the different realities in which we all are immersed, his concretion, his ideas, his clairvoyance, his coherence. . . . We could say that books like *Pedagogy of the Oppressed*, *Pedagogy of the Question*, or *Pedagogy of Hope* have been the key in shaping a perspective or dynamic of reading the world, and also writing the world and the word, and in putting this perspective into action.

## What do you think Paulo Freire would say about how his theories are used today?

From my perspective, Freire would have mixed feelings. On the one hand, the joy of seeing his "utopia", practices and theories, his way of living and doing having mushroomed in the world and society at the hands of women and men involved in processes of subjectivity and/or awareness.

On the other hand, Freire would have a certain desolation to see the fallacious use of many of his concepts in practical domestication—in universities, governments, and social movements. He also would have a certain perplexity, seeing how much of the analysis and how many of the arguments he included in *Pedagogy of the Oppressed* could be used in the present time.

## What do you think a Freirean University would look like today?

A Freirean University would have at its core the methodological action of theoretical and practical intervention, which would lead to an awakened practice and promote a participatory and collaborative culture at the university, that is, we would be at a university where the process of awareness, through dialogue and continued questioning between peers, would lead to the construction of a process of liberation. Thus, we would be able to de-apprehend those dynamics, actions, procedures that we all have internalized in order to move toward a democratic, flexible, open, common society, where we could overcome the sectarianism we are involved in as a "subject" and become thinking men, women, and children (and not oppressed subjects).

## If students took just one thing away from reading *Pedagogy of the Oppressed* what would you hope it would be?

I cannot be limited to picking just one thing. I would choose the dialogic method and emancipation method, the problem-conception of politics, ethics, and education. I would choose critical analysis of specific realities. But above all, I would choose the proposal that reading the world precedes reading the word, and both the world and the word are in constant transformation, and we are always main characters in these actions.

# Noam Chomsky

*Massachusetts Institute of Technology, USA*

**Please tell us about your background and current areas of expertise.**

Linguistics, cognitive science, philosophy.

**What do you think Paulo Freire would say about how his theories are used today?**

I think he would be generally appalled by the current teach-to-test doctrines.

**What do you think a Freirean university would look like today?**

Instruction should reject the notion of education as pouring water into a vessel (in a phrase used in the Enlightenment, Freire's "banking model"), in favor of engaging students in an active quest for understanding in a faculty-student cooperative environment. To a significant extent something like that is true of science teaching, at its best, sometimes elsewhere.

**If students took just one thing away from reading *Pedagogy of the Oppressed* what would you hope it would be?**

They should recognize that education should be a process of self-discovery, of developing one's own capacities and pursuing interests and concerns with an open and independent mind, all in cooperation with others.

# Gustavo E. Fischman

*Arizona State University, USA*

**Please tell us about your background and current areas of expertise.**

I am a professor in educational policy and director of edXchange, the knowledge mobilization initiative at the Mary Lou Fulton Teachers College, Arizona State University. I started to work in education as a popular educator in the early 1980s in Argentina without any formal training in either pedagogy or research. Popular education at that time was closely related to Freirean ideals and was oriented to work in a nonauthoritarian but guided pedagogical approach with the goal of social liberation.

**How did you come to read Freire's *Pedagogy of the Oppressed* for the first time?**

The first time I heard anything about *Pedagogy of the Oppressed* was not an invitation to read it, but an order to ignore it. In 1977, I was a 16-year-old studying industrial chemistry in a vocational school in Buenos Aires. I was not particularly politicized, but like everyone else in the country, I was acutely aware that we were living under a brutal dictatorship. It still makes me angry recalling how baffled I felt when the principal at my high school posted notes—following the guidelines of the ministry of education—announcing that the simple possession of any of the books on the list of "immoral and dangerous readings" was evidence of "terrorist sympathies" and reason enough to be expelled from the school. I remember that I became very curious that a book about education made it into this long list of "dangerous" books.

Seven years later, and in September 1984, I was a member of a popular education group, volunteering in a shanty town in Buenos Aires for an adult literacy project, when my partner told me the

International Council of Adult Education (ICAE) was looking for volunteers to organize their 1985 annual meeting. The keynote speaker was Paulo Freire, who was returning to Argentina for the first time since his books were banned in the country. I immediately volunteered to be part of the team that was organizing the meeting, and I got a used copy of *Pedagogy of the Oppressed* and began my informal education of all things Freirean.

**What do you think a Freirean university would look like today?**

Following Freire's dictum of being simple without being simplistic, a Freirean university should have three key defining characteristics. First, it should be structured to implement a pedagogy of liberation committed to the principles of freedom, equity, inclusivity, and solidarity. A pedagogy of liberation will engage in curious, rigorous, and usable teaching, service, and research agendas. Second, the students, faculty, and administration should be as diverse as their societies. Diversity in two different but related senses: serving diverse sectors and all social groups of a society as well as diversity of ideas and orientations. Third, a Freirean university will be organized as a laboratory of democratic participatory governing.

**Can you describe how, and to what extent, you think Freire's work has had an impact on pedagogy?**

I think the biggest impact of Freire's work is that it has demonstrated how even short-lived experiences of democratic schooling—in a single classroom, in or outside schools, with children or adults—are worth pursuing. These experiences teach us to not only expect more from ourselves as educators and learners but also link individual and social actions with the goals of equality and solidarity.

# Ramón Flecha

*University of Barcelona, Spain*

**Please tell us about your background and current areas of expertise.**

I am devoted to scientific research in search of both intellectual and human excellence, focusing on the identification of actions that tackle inequalities in different social fields: ethnic and minority groups; gender issues, especially in the field of masculinity studies; education; and economy, specifically focusing on organizations that are successful in overcoming income inequalities, etc. In other words, I have never been interested in the analysis of inequality by itself because I think such analysis benefits only the people who develop it. Rather, I am interested in the analysis of human actions that are actively overcoming inequalities, something that Freire appreciated very much.

**What do you think Paulo Freire would say about how his theories are used today?**

I do not know what Freire would think, but what I can say is that Freire had great intuition and was always ahead of his time. In 1969, with *Pedagogy of the Oppressed*, he had already developed a theory of dialogic action, which did not arrive in the social sciences until 1981, 12 years later, with Habermas's Theory of Communicative Action. What Freire defined as dialogic action, or dialogic perspective, is the current trend in social sciences, in the field of economics, sociology, anthropology, and political science. I think Freire would be satisfied to see how the social sciences today are in line with the dialogic perspective that he foresaw in the 1960s.

**Can you describe how, and to what extent, you think Freire's work has had an impact on research?**

I think the impact of Freire's work on research has been extremely positive. The dialogic perspective helped show that it is necessary to open a dialogue with the people who are the object of study. What happens is that the meaning of this dialogue, what dialogue meant to Freire, has often not been well understood. Research should be truly dialogic with the end-users of a given study. Although the subject may be a person working 8 hours a day in domestic cleaning, the researcher is being paid to read and study the scientific knowledge. Unfortunately, some people have understood only the "go and dialogue with the subjects" part, without doing the rest of their job, without working hard like Freire did, without reading the applicable social sciences literature so that they can use that knowledge in the dialogue with the end-users.

**Can you describe how, and to what extent, you think Freire's work has had an impact on pedagogy?**

Honestly, Freire's work has had an impressive impact worldwide. Freire is possibly the most influential scholar in education. The problem is that this influence has not always reached educational practice. For example, in universities, many people declare themselves as being Freirean, but they are not helping transform the actual conditions of the schools or the educational practices to be in line with Freirean guidelines.

**If students took just one thing away from reading *Pedagogy of the Oppressed* what would you hope it would be?**

I especially wish students would prioritize something that is forgotten in most educational systems, which is the right to education for all children. Very often, decisions are made based on reasons that are very far from the improvement of educational outcomes of all children. It is critical that students in education embrace this ethical and human commitment; this will be their real professional task.

# Ronald David Glass

*University of California, Santa Cruz, USA*

**Please tell us about your background and current areas of expertise.**

I am a radical philosopher of education whose work emanates from and within struggles for justice. I direct the UC Center for Collaborative Research for an Equitable California, and we partner with aggrieved communities to address issues in the economy, employment, education, housing, food systems, public health, and the environment. I also head a project that investigates the ethical issues in social science research.

**What do you think Paulo Freire would say about how his theories are used today?**

I had the great good fortune and honor of working in depth with Paulo Freire in 1984, when he lived with me for a month and collaborated in the social justice movement-building activities of the Adult Education Development Project. We discussed at length how his theory was being taken up in different sectors in different countries. He agreed with me that much of the "critical pedagogy" that takes place in US schools and claims Freire's theory as its basis is in truth a domestication of the radical foundation of his ideas, even as it establishes a more humane form of schooling. Education as a practice of freedom is necessarily geared into actual efforts and struggles to transform the world, and to transform our own inner selves as well (since the oppressions of the world reside in us as well as in the structures and processes of everyday life). But Freire was not a purist, in terms of either theory or practice. He was committed to doing whatever could be done in whatever open spaces could be created, so he would be happy that people the world over have found his theory useful in their own ways, in their own particular context, to move the struggle for justice forward.

## What do you think a Freirean university would look like today?

A university based in Freire's theory would be organized to address the most pressing social, economic, and political inequities. It would take direction for its research agenda from the needs of the most aggrieved communities. It would recognize the ethical and political dimensions of knowledge claims and knowledge production. It would honor multiple modalities of knowing. It would acknowledge that scholars and their disciplines and universities are themselves tainted by histories and ideologies of oppression and exploitation. It would be less concerned with credentialing experts than it would be concerned with animating curiosity, habits of disciplined critical inquiry, and a lifetime commitment to the struggle for justice.

## Can you describe how, and to what extent, you think Freire's work has had an impact on pedagogy?

I think, in the United States, Freire's work has had limited impact on pedagogy in schools. I see his theory primarily invoked as an ethical or political marker, as an indication of a teacher's intent to honor the background experiences of students. This is usually done through an (often somewhat superficial) engagement with Chapter 2 of *Pedagogy of the Oppressed* and its famous contrast between banking and dialogical or problem-posing education. This domesticated critical pedagogy certainly is more humane, provides more space for student voice and interests, and offers a counterposition to the dominant discourse and practice of pedagogy in public schools. However, this is a very limited embodiment of the theory. It is the case that some teachers, such as those organized in Teachers for Social Justice, have developed more robust embodiments of the theory, and are looking for ways to link classroom learning to larger movements seeking to effect change in the community. Freire's theory has been used pedagogically within movement building, and here it has found much stronger forms of expression, particularly in Latin America.

# Valerie Kinloch

*University of Pittsburgh, USA*

**Please tell us about your background and current areas of expertise.**

I am the Renée and Richard Goldman Dean of the School of Education at the University of Pittsburgh, where I collaborate with colleagues on important local, national, and global educational initiatives. Before being named dean, I was professor of Literacy Studies and associate dean at Ohio State University, where I facilitated initiatives on diversity and inclusion in education, international educational partnerships, and school and community engagement. My research examines the literacies and community engagements of young people and adults inside and outside schools. I am the author of publications on race, place, literacy, and diversity, and I am currently working on related research and engagement initiatives.

**How did you come to read Freire's *Pedagogy of the Oppressed* for the first time?**

I "discovered" Freire's *Pedagogy of the Oppressed* when I was an undergraduate student majoring in English at Johnson C. Smith University. I recall having countless conversations with my friends and some of my professors about black literature, black lives, oppression, and the power of language and literacy, and I was moved to continue on my journey to read various texts by black authors and scholars. In one of those texts, the idea of "reading the word and the world" was presented to me, and when I searched for the meaning of the phrase, Paulo Freire's name and book came up. So, I read *Pedagogy of the Oppressed* and fell in love with his discussion of critical consciousness and connections that should happen among teachers, students, and the world.

**What do you think a Freirean university would look like today?**

I think it would include open spaces for people to engage with others, to analyze events going on in the world, to examine ways to combat oppression and inequity, to dismantle racism, classism, sexism, inequality, and capitalism. It would be free! Open to everyone. It would be guided by the need to create and enhance our stances, dispositions, and ideologies related to critical consciousness, collaborating with others, working for necessary sociopolitical change, and thinking beyond the self. It would be a humanizing, culturally rich academic space.

**Can you describe how, and to what extent, you think Freire's work has had an impact on research?**

To this day, Freire continues to push scholars to consider the complicated ways identities and locations need to be nuanced in discussions about education; he encourages us to take a critical perspective, especially when collaborating with other people in community contexts, as we attempt to address pervasive questions about inequality. He also situates research within the reach of the everyday—the everyday realities, lives, lived conditions, struggles, and hope of people—to make research accessible to who we are working with and writing with/about in our research. Thus, research is not singularly about publishing articles and books, but about writing new ways of being into existence that can, fundamentally, change the world for the better.

**If students took just one thing away from reading *Pedagogy of the Oppressed* what would you hope it would be?**

I hope it would be this: Freire's (1971) insistence that we work to eradicate systems of oppression "so that [students] can become 'beings for themselves'" as opposed to students being forced to "'integrate' into the structure of oppression" (p. 55). I believe his focus on transforming systems of oppression points to all systems—schools, universities, and political systems that we live under in our specific contexts. It also speaks to the need for us to work in solidarity to revolutionize and transform the world.

# Peter Mayo

*University of Malta, Malta*

**Please tell us about your background and current areas of expertise.**

I was brought up in Malta where I worked as a part-time journalist for a few years, then took up teaching and eventually the academic life after having pursued postgraduate studies at the University of Alberta and OISE/University of Toronto in Canada. I specialize in Sociology of Education with a focus on Adult Education and have also been involved in university outreach developing projects that have their basis in issues and commemorations that capture community members' imagination and are therefore rooted in popular consciousness.

**How did you come to read Freire's *Pedagogy of the Oppressed* for the first time?**

The occasion for reading *Pedagogy of the Oppressed* presented itself at the start of my graduate studies in Edmonton, Alberta and the book certainly proved a revelation to me. It seemed to contain many of the insights and elements necessary for me to understand the context in which my previous teaching in Malta had taken place. These included subalterneity, colonial legacies, relative poverty, class issues (including language issues), and issues concerning racism (there were African-Maltese students in our school at a time when Maltese society was nowhere near the multiethnic society it has become in recent times).

**What do you think a Freirean university would look like today?**

It would be one wherein the institution and the education it provides are conceived of as public goods, not consumption goods. It would be one where engagement with the community would be given central importance. It would be one where the starting point for learning is the students' existential situation with knowledge deriving from thematic complexes researched within and emerging from the community. It would be one in which the transmission model of lecturing is replaced by co-investigation, involving lecturers, students and community members, debating issues which are raised in a manner that arouses "epistemological curiosity" and becomes the object of collective enquiry.

**Can you describe how, and to what extent, you think Freire's work has had an impact on research?**

The greatest Freirean impact on research can be felt in that approach known as Participatory Action Research, a collective form of research where community members are assisted in researching issues that affect their own and surrounding lives. I would argue that Freire has a lot to tell us about the ethics of research and the extent to which those whose lives and issues are being examined are genuinely involved in determining the research agenda and research process. They would benefit from co-ownership of the entire research process and its outcomes. This research process and outcome should serve to improve their ways of life. It is a value-committed effort which affirms the choice and purposes of research in line with the view that knowledge and research are not neutral. In short it is research geared not simply to interpret the world but primarily to contribute toward changing it.

**Can you describe how, and to what extent, you think Freire's work has had an impact on pedagogy?**

Freire has inspired many to move away from a hierarchical, magisterial mode of teaching and learning to a more democratic approach, an approach built on the teacher's democratic authority which does not degenerate into authoritarianism. He has also inspired educators to recognize the politics of education and knowledge, to eschew any pretense of neutrality, and most important of all, he has emphasized the collective dimensions of learning and the need to start from the learners' existential situations, with all their differences, and move to higher orders of learning and knowledge.

# Peter McLaren

*Chapman University, USA*

**Please tell us about your background and current areas of expertise.**

I served as an elementary school teacher in Toronto's Jane-Finch Corridor, a public housing district in Canada known for its high rate of crime. I earned a hard-won reputation for successfully teaching working class immigrants.

I subsequently applied for and was accepted into a PhD program in education at the University of Toronto, during which time I published the diary I had kept as an elementary school teacher. I called it *Cries from the Corridor* and it became a Canadian best-seller in 1980. After I had finished a grueling national book tour, I was already growing self-critical about the fact that *Cries from the Corridor* was woefully absent of a theoretical framework that could help readers understand the violence and alienation experienced by students in my classroom. Progressive and radial educators alike had for decades winced in gut churning unison at the tellingly restrained efforts to take seriously educational reform throughout the country, establishing a bog-standard evasion for challenging seriously the role that education plays in the reproduction of the asymmetrical relations of power and privilege of the capitalist state and I feared that my book was not sufficiently helpful in deepening an understanding of capitalist schooling. To remedy both the calculated indifference of educational officials as well as my insufficiently developed theoretical center of gravity, I began to read across disciplines, shifting my early interest in Chaucer, Beowulf, Shakespeare and Blake towards an incorporation of the sociology of knowledge, anthropology, critical theory, and semiotics. I took the time to audit courses with Michel Foucault, Umberto Eco, Ernesto Laclau and other visiting intellectuals. I finally graduated with my doctorate in 1984, still feeling that there was so much to learn.

My doctoral dissertation was published as a book, *Schooling as a Ritual Performance*, and to my great excitement Professor Henry Giroux agreed to write the Preface. Henry became a mentor to me and invited me to join him at Miami University of Ohio as a fellow professor. Henry introduced me to one of his best friends, Donaldo Macedo, from whom I learned a great deal about Paulo Freire and his work. Henry arranged for me to meet Paulo in 1985 and I was surprised— no, shocked—to learn that Paulo was already familiar with my work. In fact, he would refer to me as his "intellectual cousin" and a part of his pedagogical family. In the ensuing years he was gracious enough to write prefaces for two of my books and an endorsement for a third. In subsequent years until his death he exhibited a soulful kindness toward me and my ongoing project of developing critical pedagogy in North American—and later primarily Latin American and Asian—contexts.

### How did you come to read Freire's *Pedagogy of the Oppressed* for the first time?

I read *Pedagogy of the Oppressed* while a doctoral student in Toronto. It was not on any required reading lists in my classes but friends of mine on the left pronounced it as a must-read work so I read it in conjunction with other educators and social and political theorists that I was reading at the time. Paulo's work stood out for its relevance to my own life experiences both as a student and as an educator, dramatically so. It helped to sharpen my understanding of praxis, and the necessity for engaging in social struggles and then returning to theoretical and philosophical works for clarification and for deepening my understanding of those experiences.

### What do you think Paulo Freire would say about how his theories are used today?

I think Paulo, in all of his great humility, would be appreciative that his work has made such a powerful impact on so many fields and that it has become such a powerful antidote to prevailing forms of social and polictical amnesia and to the motivated forget fulness that surrounds the foundational violence of all societies. But I also believe that he would be critical of approaches in education that claimed to be Freirean but which domesticated his work, leeching from its foundations a radical politics that was critical of capitalism and which could certainly be called socialist.

**What do you think a Freirean university would look like today?**

A Freirean university in the North American context would be centered around the elimination of economic inequality and social relations of oppression related to sexuality, age, species, gender, white supremacy, and the coloniality of power, all of which are related in different ways to the unequal ownership of capital and to capitalist value production itself and the exploitation, alienation, and logic of abstraction that accompanies it. The unequal ownership of capital cannot be remedied by higher growth rates within the conceptual models of neoclassical economics but only by transcending capitalism through a socialist alternative. The Freirean University will be about rebuilding public sectors, democratizing the workplace, establishing communal councils that are committed to models of participatory and direct democracy, eliminating race, class and gender antagonisms, creating a revolutionary critical humanism that transcends private property and that is committed to creating communities of engaged learners and Freely associated laborers dedicated to working in the interests of a truly global commons.

**Can you describe how, and to what extent, you think Freire's work has had an impact on research?**

Freire's work has had a strikingly significant impact on the genesis and ongoing development of the field of critical pedagogy. Critical pedagogy is constituted by a body of theory associated with Freire's work and critical social theory more generally that emphasizes praxis. The field of critical pedagogy has recently expanded its purview to include revolutionary critical pedagogy, an attempt to reclaim Freire's Marxist epistemological roots through the development of a philosophy of praxis driven primarily by the work of Marx Hegel and humanist philosophers. Freire's research has been felt in the fields of theology, literacy, composition studies, literary studies, applied linguistics, sociology, anthropology, and political philosophy. That his work has cross-fertilized so many areas of research is a testament to its transdisciplinary reach in the service of a truly decolonial pedagogy of hope and self and social transformation.

**If students took just one thing away from reading *Pedagogy of the Oppressed* what would you hope it would be?**

It would be that they would never just take one thing away from reading Paulo Freire but realize that their everyday lives always have pedagogical dimensions to them, and those pedagogical dimensions are, in turn and at one and the same time, political dimensions that challenge our obligation to the poor, the immiserated, and the dispossessed, that sharpen our antological and epistemological clarity and that challenge our commitment to building a better world, free from unnecessary alienation and human suffering.

# Margo Okazawa-Rey

*San Francisco State University, USA and*
*Fielding Graduate University, USA*

**Please tell us about your background and current areas of expertise.**

My primary areas of work—teaching, research, and activism—focus on militarism, armed conflict, and violence against women. I have examined the connections between militarism, economic globalization, and impacts on local and migrant women in South Korea who live and work around US military bases. I have conducted feminist activist research methodology training sessions with women activists in the Niger Delta region, Ghana, Sierra Leone, and Liberia. I use popular education in community settings to conduct antiracist and multicultural workshops and in my undergraduate and graduate courses.

**How did you come to read Freire's *Pedagogy of the Oppressed* for the first time?**

In the late 1970s, a small group of feminist activists in Boston, USA began to read and learn from *Pedagogy of the Oppressed* together, striving to understand and create radical methodologies for living, understanding, and teaching the feminist slogan, "the personal is political." What better way than through ideas we learned from Freire? We did not realize before that the feminist consciousness-raising groups were based on, or at least unknowingly related to, his work. The writing was turgid and we were sometimes challenged by masculinist language of "he," "him," and "men." Nonetheless, we carried on—to our enormous benefit.

**What do you think Paulo Freire would say about how his theories are used today?**

I had the honor of meeting Freire in person in the 1980s and was struck by his unpretentiousness, his simplicity. So, I believe he would be surprised, pleasantly, by the extensive use of his work by a range of educators around the world. He also would be seriously concerned and dismayed by the distortion and debasement of key ideas like starting from students' experiences—reading the world to read the word—to technocratic concepts like "learner-centered" that have come to mean "you students can have some say in what you learn but we teachers still control the curriculum." Perhaps more important, the liberatory purpose of education that Freire so consistently articulated and rearticulated has been left to one side on the way to increasingly mechanized learning and teaching contexts in public education for primary, secondary, and tertiary students.

Freire would delight truly at the uptake of his work in places similar to where he began—rural areas of the world including in "developed" countries like the United States—where peasants and working-class folk with and without literacy skills are learning to analyze, understand, and change the conditions that oppress and marginalize them.

**What do you think a Freirean university would look like today?**

"Freirean University" would be an oxymoron today. The forces of neoliberalism and conservatism that have engulfed most universities would result in the same harm being inflicted currently, irrespective of a name change. The most radical educational settings that could faithfully apply and advance Freire's work would be in informal settings, what I refer to as "free spaces," including activist movements, and within formal settings like universities, where we could learn and teach together as we face material and social conditions that are so heavily and horrifically shaping our lives and recognize our shared destinies, oppressed and oppressor, dominant and subordinate, the vocal and the silent and silenced.

**Can you describe how, and to what extent, you think Freire's work has had an impact on research?**

Liberatory methodologies that I am most familiar with—feminist and decolonizing—are rooted in Freirean, feminist, and indigenous epistemologies and research methods. I have experienced how Paulo Freire's theories have been applied creatively and convincingly in both.

# Foreword to the Original English Edition (1970)

Richard Shaull

Over the years, the thought and work of the Brazilian educator Paulo Freire have spread from the North East of Brazil to an entire continent, and have made a profound impact not only in the field of education but also in the overall struggle for national development. At the precise moment when the disinherited masses in Latin America are awakening from their traditional lethargy and are anxious to participate, as Subjects, in the development of their countries, Paulo Freire has perfected a method for teaching illiterates that has contributed, in an extraordinary way, to that process. In fact, those who, in learning to read and write, come to a new awareness of selfhood and begin to look critically at the social situation in which they find themselves, often take the initiative in acting to transform the society that has denied them this opportunity of participation. Education is once again a subversive force.

In this country, we are gradually becoming aware of the work of Paulo Freire, but thus far we have thought of it primarily in terms of its contribution to the education of illiterate adults in the Third World. If, however, we take a closer look, we may discover that his methodology as well as his educational philosophy are as important for us as for the dispossessed in Latin America. Their struggle to become free Subjects and to participate in the transformation of their society is similar, in many ways, to the struggle not only of blacks and Mexican-Americans but also of middle-class young people in this country. And the sharpness and intensity of that struggle in the developing world may well provide us with new insight, new models, and a new hope as we face our own situation. For this reason, I consider the publication of *Pedagogy of the Oppressed* in an English edition to be something of an event.

Paulo Freire's thought represents the response of a creative mind and sensitive conscience to the extraordinary misery and suffering of the oppressed around him. Born in 1921 in Recife, the center of one of the most extreme situations of poverty and underdevelopment in the Third World, he was soon forced to experience that reality directly. As the economic crisis in 1929 in the United States began to affect Brazil, the precarious stability of Freire's middle-class family gave way and he found himself sharing the plight of the "wretched of the earth." This had a profound influence on his life as he came to know the gnawing pangs of hunger and fell behind in school because of the listlessness it produced; it also led him to make a vow, at age eleven, to dedicate his life to the struggle against hunger, so that other children would not have to know the agony he was then experiencing.

His early sharing of the life of the poor also led him to the discovery of what he describes as the "culture of silence" of the dispossessed. He came to realize that their ignorance and lethargy were the direct product of the whole situation of economic, social, and political domination—and of the paternalism—of which they were victims. Rather than being encouraged and equipped to know and respond to the concrete realities of their world, they were kept "submerged" in a situation in which such critical awareness and response were practically impossible. And it became clear to him that the whole educational system was one of the major instruments for the maintenance of this culture of silence.

Confronted by this problem in a very existential way, Freire turned his attention to the field of education and began to work on it. Over the years, he has engaged in a process of study and reflection that has produced something quite new and creative in educational philosophy. From a situation of direct engagement in the struggle to liberate men and women for the creation of a new world, he has reached out to the thought and experience of those in many different situations and of diverse philosophical positions: in his words, to "Sartre and Mounier, Erich Fromm and Louis Althusser, Ortega y Gasset and Mao, Martin Luther King and Che Guevara, Unamuno and Marcuse." He has made use of the insights of these men to develop a perspective on education which is authentically his own and which seeks to respond to the concrete realities of Latin America.

His thought on the philosophy of education was first expressed in 1959 in his doctoral dissertation at the University of Recife, and later in his work as Professor of the History and Philosophy of Education in the same university, as well as in his early experiments with the teaching of illiterates in that same city. The methodology he developed was widely used by Catholics and others in literacy campaigns throughout the North East of Brazil, and was considered such a threat to the old order that Freire was jailed immediately after the military coup in 1964. Released seventy days later and encouraged to leave the country, Freire went to Chile, where he spent five years working with UNESCO and the Chilean Institute for Agrarian Reform in programs of adult education. He then acted as a consultant at Harvard University's School of Education, and worked in close association with a number of groups engaged in new educational experiments in rural and urban areas. He is presently serving as Special Consultant to the Office of Education of the World Council of Churches in Geneva.

Freire has written many articles in Portuguese and Spanish, and his first book, *Educação como Prática da Liberdade,* was published in Brazil in 1967. His latest and most complete work, *Pedagogy of the Oppressed,* is the first of his writings to be published in this country.

In this brief introduction, there is no point in attempting to sum up, in a few paragraphs, what the author develops in a number of pages. That would be an offense to the richness, depth, and complexity of his thought. But perhaps a word of witness has its place here—a personal witness as to why I find a dialogue with the thought of Paulo Freire an exciting adventure. Fed up as I am with the abstractness and sterility of so much intellectual work in academic circles today, I am excited by a process of reflection which is set in a thoroughly historical context, which is carried on in the midst of a struggle to create a new social order and thus represents a new unity of theory and *praxis*. And I am encouraged when a man of the stature of Paulo Freire incarnates a rediscovery of the humanizing vocation of the intellectual, and demonstrates the power of thought to negate accepted limits and open the way to a new future.

Freire is able to do this because he operates on one basic assumption: that man's ontological vocation (as he calls it) is to be a Subject who acts upon and transforms his world, and in so doing moves toward ever new possibilities of fuller and richer life individually and collectively. This *world* to which he relates is not a static and closed order, a *given* reality which man must accept and to which he must adjust; rather, it is a problem to be worked on and solved. It is the material used by man to create history, a task which he performs as he overcomes that which is dehumanizing at any particular time and place and dares to create the qualitatively new. For Freire, the resources for that task at the present time are provided by the advanced technology of our Western world, but the social vision which impels us to negate the present order and demonstrate that history has not ended comes primarily from the suffering and struggle of the people of the Third World.

Coupled with this is Freire's conviction (now supported by a wide background of experience) that every human being, no matter how "ignorant" or submerged in the "culture of silence" he or she may be, is capable of looking critically at the world in a dialogical encounter with others. Provided with the proper tools for such encounter, the individual can gradually perceive personal and social reality as well as the contradictions in it, become conscious of his or her own perception of that reality, and deal critically with it. In this process, the old, paternalistic teacher-student relationship is overcome. A peasant can facilitate this process for a neighbor more effectively than a "teacher" brought in from outside. "People educate each other through the mediation of the world."

As this happens, the word takes on new power. It is no longer an abstraction or magic but a means by which people discover themselves and their potential as they give names to things around them. As Freire puts it, each individual wins back the right to *say his or her own word, to name the world.*

When an illiterate peasant participates in this sort of educational experience, he or she comes to a new awareness of self, has a new sense of dignity, and is stirred by a new hope. Time and again, peasants have expressed these discoveries in striking ways after a few hours of class: "I now realize I am a person, an educated person." "We were blind, now our eyes have been opened." "Before this, words meant nothing to me; now they speak to me and I can make them speak." "Now we will no longer be a dead weight on the cooperative farm." When this happens in the process of learning to read, men and women discover that they are creators of culture, and that all their work can be creative. "I work, and working I transform the world." And as those who have been completely marginalized are so radically transformed, they are no longer willing to be mere objects, responding to changes occurring around them; they are more likely to decide to take upon themselves the struggle to change the structures of society, which until now have served to oppress them. For this reason, a distinguished Brazilian student of national development recently affirmed that this type of educational work among the people represents a new factor in social change and development, "a new instrument of conduct for the Third World, by which it can overcome traditional structures and enter the modern world."

At first sight, Paulo Freire's method of teaching illiterates in Latin America seems to belong to a different world from that in which we find ourselves in this country. Certainly, it would be absurd to claim that it should be copied here. But there are certain parallels in the two situations that should not be overlooked. Our advanced technological society is rapidly making objects of most of us and subtly programming us into conformity to the logic of its system. To the degree that this happens, we are also becoming submerged in a new "culture of silence."

The paradox is that the same technology that does this to us also creates a new sensitivity to what is happening. Especially among young people, the new media together with the erosion of old concepts of authority open the way to acute awareness of this new bondage. The young perceive that their right to say their own word has been stolen from them, and that few things are more important than the struggle to win it back. And they also realize that the educational system today—from kindergarten to university—is their enemy.

There is no such thing as a *neutral* educational process. Education either functions as an instrument that is used to facilitate the integration of the younger generation into the logic of the present system and bring about conformity to it, *or* it becomes "the practice of freedom," the means by which men and women deal critically and creatively with reality and discover how to participate in the transformation of their world. The development of an educational methodology that facilitates this process will inevitably lead to tension and conflict within our society. But it could also contribute to the formation of a new man and mark the beginning of a new era in Western history. For those who are committed to that task and are searching for concepts and tools for experimentation, Paulo Freire's thought will make a significant contribution in the years ahead.